SAINT OF AUSCHWITZ

C000280199

By the same author

Backward Christian Soldiers (Hutchinson)
Orphans of the Living (Hutchinson)
All for Christ (Oxford University Press)

SAINT OF AUSCHWITZ

*The Story of
Maksymilian Kolbe*

Diana Dewar

DARTON, LONGMAN AND TODD
London

First published in 1982
Darton, Longman and Todd Ltd
89 Lillie Road, London SW6 1UD

Reprinted 1983

© 1982 Diana Dewar

ISBN 0 232 51574 3

British Library Cataloguing in Publication Data

Dewar, Diana
  Saint of Auschwitz.
  1. Kolbe, Maksymilian   2. Catholics—Poland
  —Biography
  I. Title
  282'.092'4   BX4705.K/

  ISBN 0-232-51574-3

Phototypset by Input Typesetting Ltd, London SW19 8DR
Printed in Great Britain by The Anchor Press Ltd
and bound by Wm Brendon & Son Ltd
both of Tiptree Essex

For Stephen, with love

'A victory through faith and love was won by him in this place, which was built for the negation of faith – faith in God and faith in man – and to trample radically not only on love but on all signs of human dignity, of humanity.'

Pope John Paul II, Oświęcim (Auschwitz)
7 June 1979

CONTENTS

ILLUSTRATIONS

(between pages 82 and 83)

Thanks are due to Bay Books of Kensington, New South Wales, for permission to reproduce plates 8 and 9 and to Popperfoto for permission to reproduce plate 10.

ACKNOWLEDGEMENTS

I owe the greatest debt to the Friars of Niepokalanów who gave me their recollections and where I was privileged to use the copious collection of documents. I also experienced true Franciscan hospitality.

I deeply appreciate the courtesy and help of Mr Franciszek Gajowniczek and his wife, Helena.

My affectionate thanks are due to my interpreter in Warsaw and my translator in Bristol, both of whom brought so much diligence and patience to the task.

I am much indebted to Dr Antony Polonsky for giving generously of his time to advise me on details of Polish history. For help in tracing survivors of Auschwitz I am grateful to Dr Józef Garliński, whose knowledge of the camps was invaluable.

May I also record my thanks to Fr John Burdyszek, Fr Cornelian Dende, Sister Lorna Francis (Society of the Sacred Cross), Fr Giorgio M. Domanski, Fr Bernard M. Geiger, Fr Lucian Królikowski, Fr Gerard McCann, Fr Paul Przybylski, Fr James Scott, Mr Peter Spicer, and Fr Theresianus Sueyoshi.

I am grateful too, to the staff of the Avon County Library, Bristol University Library, The Catholic Central Library, The Institute of Jewish Affairs and The Polish Library.

Most of all, my thanks go to James, my husband, and Stephen, my youngest son, for much help and encouragement.

CHAPTER ONE

In the early spring of 1981 twenty divisions of Russian troops were reported to be patrolling Poland's borders in aggrandized and prolonged Warsaw Pact manoeuvres, code-named Soyuz 81. The fledgling free trade union, 'Solidarity', threatened a general strike over an incident at Bydgoszcz in which police were alleged to have assaulted union activists. The world's media called in experts on Eastern Europe to conjecture on Soviet policy and suspense mounted. The invasion scare revived. On 31 March 'Solidarity' called off its total strike threat after talks with the Government which preceded important concessions. 'Rural Solidarity' for independent landowners became recognized, and 'Solidarity' was given radio and television time and allowed to print its own newspaper. A two months' moratorium on strikes was agreed in the interests of a modicum of stability.

I took advantage of this opportunity and flew to Poland to research this book. None of my fellow-passengers looked like British holiday-makers; most were homeward-bound Poles and some wore the red and white 'Solidarność' badge in their lapels. The air hostess looked at me curiously as if inviting a reason for my journey: after all, Poland was not the place for a halcyon holiday. The country was in a state of high tension and economic chaos, food was short and there were queues for almost everything. I smiled in reply to her unspoken question and returned to my *Polish for Travellers* to learn, at least, the courtesy words.

I hesitated to tell her the purpose of my visit because I doubted if she would believe me, and anyway, it might have sounded awesome. I would have had to say that I was a

1

pilgrim in search of a saint, a modern saint: Maksymilian Maria Kolbe, died 1941, beatified 1971, and canonized in 1982. He was a Catholic priest, and a Franciscan, who gave his life for another man at Auschwitz. (Perhaps the young hostess would not have heard of Auschwitz.) Ten men were condemned to die in a starvation bunker and Kolbe took the place of a younger man who was married and had a family. I wanted to meet that man to learn what he has done with his life. I wanted to meet the friars at the community Kolbe founded near Warsaw and which by 1939 had become one of the biggest friaries in the world. Once it had also printed papers read by millions and I wanted to discover the secrets of an editor who could launch a national daily when other newspapers were made bankrupt by the Depression. I wanted to visit Auschwitz, which Pope John Paul II described as 'the Golgotha of the modern world'. Moreover I wanted 'to breathe' everything Polish, absorb the sights and sounds and scents of Poland; for to begin to understand the saints, like the poets, you must know something of their country.

I was beginning to think my journey foolish. I am not a Catholic, I know no Polish, and I had been able to make only vague arrangements for an interpreter. I had been told that there was one friar with workable English at the monastery and one whose English was excellent, but whose time was largely taken up teaching in the minor seminary. A friend of a friend at the Polish Church in Bristol, where I live, had been asked to help, and I had telephoned her in Warsaw. She promised to do her best. One of her family, probably her uncle, would try to meet me; she could not do so herself because she was nursing her dying mother.

I began to feel apprehensive. My visa was in order – I had been frank about my intentions and so it had taken weeks rather than days to get it – but supposing the Customs confiscated my tapes or notebooks? Would the uncle of my friend's friend recognize me? I put on one red glove, a prearranged identification, rather ridiculous but effective: it was a warm day and no one was wearing gloves of any colour let

2

alone bright red. If no one met me, would I manage to find my way to the friary, *Niepokalanów*, which means The City of the Immaculate? It is not on any map of Poland but lies some forty-two kilometres west of Warsaw. Supposing the friar's English was passable, but inadequate for the exacting demands of a biographer? Had the friend's friend been able to find anyone to help me?

I do not record these difficulties in order to invite readers to think me brave and resourceful. Far from it, I felt lacking both confidence and competence, but I wish to illustrate the extraordinary compulsion I felt to make this journey around Kolbe, despite my blatant lack of qualifications as an English-woman, a non-linguist, and an Anglican. I did not intend to produce a definitive book but to write as a journalist, to follow a compelling story. It was, if you like, an act of journalistic faith, and it was to be rewarded by abundant kindness.

Thankfully, the Customs had no interest in my 'hardware' – recorder, tapes and batteries. I looked around anxiously to see if anyone was going to hail me, when to my delight I saw a placard held against the railings, saying 'Welcome to Poland Diana Dewar'. It was displayed by an elderly gentleman with a beard whose woman companion held a posy of flowers of the fragrant old-fashioned kind. Both smiled and waved. It was a charming welcome. He was the 'uncle', and she the 'reserve', if the translation facilities were lacking. She explained diffidently that she did not wish to hurt the feelings of the friars, but if I liked, she would come with me. She did not want payment, she would do it for the sake of Father Kolbe. She became a good friend who was to bring much sensitivity to her task over the next two weeks.

Firstly we drove to the niece's house where she awaited us with coffee, pretzels and chocolates. (I was soon to realize these delights must have come from a foreign food parcel.) I gave her jellies and custard powders and she was touchingly grateful; she wanted them for her old mother who was dying. I delved into my bag – it was crammed with small gifts and a few clothes – and gave 'uncle' a half bottle of whisky. He drove me and my new-found interpreter to Niepokalanów.

It was much as I had imagined, set in flat agreeable countryside in which, as in Holland, you are much aware of the wide-spreading skies. Friars were chatting with the coachloads of pilgrims who came from all over the country to visit the huge basilica, an exhibition on the life of Kolbe, and a panorama depicting a Millennium of Christianity in Poland.

Brother Cornelius, a warm man with a strong handshake, met us, and it was apparent he had been delegated to look after us throughout our stay. He took these duties to heart. Not only did he bring copious documents from the archives and lead a succession of brother to us to give their fond recollections of Maksymilian; but like a cheerful conjurer he produced apples and biscuits from the capacious folds of his habit. 'Please take them, I know you're used to bigger meals', he said.

The friars could not wait to talk about Father Kolbe. As a woman I was not allowed to enter their enclosure (Brother Cornelius told me that a woman had once dressed as a man to get inside the friary but her disguise was quickly penetrated), so they came to my small room in the guest wing.

They were an impressive and endearing fraternity, and despite their common purpose and discipline, each his own man with a distinctive contribution to bring. Brother Arnold, Father Kolbe's official secretary, a scholarly and scrupulous man whose remarks were always well-considered, had the job after the war of collecting and collating much of the evidence for the beatification. He was gently caustic about some of the pilgrims who would ask to lie on Kolbe's bed: 'I suppose they think if it were a hard bed, he was a great saint; if a soft bed, a lesser saint.' He was careful to caution me about some of the glosses, the embroideries, and to remind me sensibly that some of the reminiscences might be a little less than accurate simply because of the passing of fifty-odd years.

Brother Hieronim had spent fifty years at Niepokalanów, a quiet intensely sincere man who took his time to select those

4

incidents which had impressed him most. Brother Gabriel, whose name is apposite, painted an affectionate picture of Maksymilian, not as a suffering priest but as a cheerful volcano of a man with gigantic plans to change the world. Brother Henryk transported me to the Japanese Mission, poetically called 'The Garden of the Immaculate'. Here, although the brothers urged him to have the mission in the centre, Kolbe chose a site in the lee of a mountain, an inconvenient way out of town; but when the atomic bomb was dropped 'The Garden' was virtually unscathed and no one killed because of the protection afforded by the steep ridge. One of the first brother-firemen, Brother Cherubin, a big soldierly man at one time in the Cavalry, told me with immense pride of Niepokalanów's Fire Brigade. The golden jubilee of the Brigade had recently been celebrated by a programme on Polish Television, largely thanks to new and fragile freedoms won by the now suspended movement 'Solidarity'. Nor must I forget Brother Innocenty, the archivist for Kolbe's Militia of the Immaculate (M.I.), a crusade which was to grow into a world-wide movement. It was proscribed by the Government in 1949 and in the fifties and sixties members were sometimes harassed for wearing the M.I. brooch. He brought along the record books and was overjoyed to find I was interested not only in the statistics but the spirit behind them.

The abiding influence of Kólbe still lights this strong community and the love they have for this man who is now a saint shone from the eyes of the brothers as they talked about him. Many remembered their happiness in his company. One put it in these words, 'We particularly enjoyed our free time with him . . . he was a positive person . . . we had a good feeling just to be around him.' He too, had loved them as a father; he looked upon their vocations as God's 'precious gifts' entrusted to his care. His task he saw as making Niepokalanów 'a school for saints', and he never tired of telling the brothers, 'Sanctity is simple – a mere duty according to Christ's teaching'.

The impact of Kolbe's words and deeds came sharply into focus for me in two chance encounters in the guest wing with men who had numbers tattooed on their forearms and M.I. emblems on their lapels. One was a bank clerk, a slim fit-looking man in spite of years endured in concentration camps. Władysław Konarski thanked *me* for the British Red Cross parcels they had received and told me how Kolbe's articles had helped give him the spiritual strength to survive the camps. For me he also illustrates how the Polish brand of religion, helped by the freshly blowing winds of change, forms strong men. A year ago or so he and his colleagues *asked* the manager at the bank if they could put up the cross on the wall: he would not allow it. This year they had gone to him again and *told* him that they were hanging the cross.

The other meeting was with Tadeusz 'Teddy' Pietrzy-kowski, top professional boxer in Poland pre-war. This was the only man I was to meet personally who had known Kolbe in the camp and I give his story later. Suffice to say here that Teddy recognized Kolbe's whole conduct was extraordinary, not only his final sacrifice. 'He showed an irrational kindness, a crazy courage.' Teddy had heard about Kolbe before the war, 'about Niepokalanów, the "miraculous medal", the "Rycerz Niepokalanej". But I was so occupied with school and sports, I had no time for these things . . . Now everybody in Poland has heard about Fr Kolbe and say he's a saint . . . of course such a man draws more people into the Church.'

You shared a good feeling of community in the guest dining-room where a wall mural in pastels shows a gentle Christ breaking bread. There was much friendliness if frugal fare. For breakfast you had bread and dripping or delicious white unsalted butter. Our staple diet comprised broth, salt fish, potatoes, polony, pickled cucumbers, country cheese and home-baked bread. It was like a large family with many comings and goings and when people left the table it was customary to murmur *dziękuję* (thank you), and they were not thanking the cook or the host but each other for the simple pleasure of eating together.

These visitors, Poles and pilgrims from other countries, seemed mostly the simple hardworking Catholics Father Kolbe aimed to teach through his publications. He saw the Press as a big canon in his campaign, the Mission for Mary, and he proved an extraordinarily successful publisher. Millions of poor Polish people read Niepokalanów's publications. By 1939 the circulation of the monthly review, *Rycerz Niepokalanej*, begun in 1922, had passed a million, and his national newspaper *Mały Dziennik*, launched in 1935, 230,000 daily with eleven editions. A Latin quarterly for priests of all nationalities had a circulation of forty thousand, and half a dozen other specialist publications were produced. Not only did people read these journals in such astonishing numbers, but thousands wrote to the editors about their spiritual and material problems. Sixty-five brothers worked in the correspondence bureau set up in the 'City' to answer more than three quarters of a million letters a year, which came from all over the world, mostly from Polish emigrants. Brother Cornelius helped to reply to these letters and recalls that the social problems and injustices they presented outnumbered spiritual difficulties. Many were about poverty, slum housing, factory conditions and unemployment.

The publications achieved the declared aim of their editor-in-chief Maksymilian Kolbe, a mass readership, but they did not escape sharp and specific criticism. In some quarters it was alleged that the journals were poorly produced and that the contents were sometimes anti-semitic, naively written and without intellectual depth.

The most serious charge, of course, was the one of anti-semitism, and no doubt on occasions it could be substantiated. No editor-in-chief of a fast-expanding publishing house could conceivably read every article before publication, especially if he were also foreign missionary. Maksymilian had to delegate because he was often away from Poland. The six years, 1930 to 1936, that he spent in Japan and the Far East meant that he was out of the country for the birth of the national daily.

One of the friars Brother Hieronim, who impressed me by his sincerity and detail of his recollections, told how Father Kolbe had once summoned a meeting of his journalists to rebuke them for certain anti-semitic articles. He was travelling and so had only read these contributions when they were in print. His orders at this editorial conference were memorable: nothing must be printed unless it could carry the by-line of the Immaculate, his favourite name for Mary. Yet lingering damage was done to Father Kolbe's reputation. Brother Hieronim was in Bonn after the war, attending a session of the German Parliament, when he was approached by a stranger who told him boldly, 'I do not believe that Father Kolbe can be beatified'. 'Why?', asked Brother Hieronim. 'Because he was against the Jews', the German replied, and he supported this assertion by reference to some articles in the *Mały Dziennik*. Brother Hieronim explained that Father Kolbe had not been directly responsible and had reproved the journalists concerned.

I asked our personal host, Brother Cornelius, about Father Kolbe's attitude to the Jews. He replied in his forthright manner, 'Father Kolbe would say that the Jews are clever and there is nothing wrong with that; we want to teach the Poles to be clever too'.

Father John Burdyszek, who introduced Kolbe's Militia to England in 1952, – it expanded rapidly from a single notice in the *Catholic Herald* – was at Niepokalanów in the 'thirties, and confirmed Brother Cornelius' remarks. In Poland between the world wars ten per cent of the population were Jews – the largest proportion of Jews anywhere after America – who excelled in industry and commerce. Father Kolbe wanted the Poles to compete in business by applying modern management methods and to put just prices on their goods.

To get a more distanced appraisal, while in Cracow I talked to Marek Skwarnicki, the editor of a Catholic weekly newspaper, *Tygodnik Powszechy*, who writes under the pen-name of 'Spodek' (Polish for saucer). He said that the Church in pre-war Poland was viewed as conservative, reactionary and anti-semitic, and had strong links with the National Democrats. (Roman Dmowski, the founder of this Party, called himself a democrat but was opposed to liberal democracy as known in the West because he believed it was dominated by Jewish-Masonic influences.) Before the war 'Spodek' recalled that Jewish 'jokes' proliferated in Polish culture. They were like Irish or Scottish jokes which abound in England and had little meaning. Polish Jewish jokes depicted a stereotype who was to some extent funny because he showed wisdom and not stupidity. Pre-war the Jews controlled much of the business life of Poland and for many it was a time when Poles were not in favour of having shops, and trade was generally despised as being somehow parasitic and unproductive.

The ascendancy of the Jewish business community was not to last. 'Spodek' dismissed Jewish jokes as meaningless and harmless; but there was pitiable poverty among the Jews in Poland immediately before the last war because of growing anti-semitism. The Government opposed anti-Jewish violence but saw nothing wrong with boycotting their businesses, and ruined countless Jewish traders by refusing to offer a moratorium on their debts although in 1933 it had authorized one to peasants who owed money. Government-sponsored peasant co-operatives by-passed Jewish middlemen and Jews were practically excluded from Poland's timber trade in which, among many other trades, they had been prominent. The Government allowed restrictions on the entry of Jews into trade schools and the universities and also began to refuse to recognize professional qualifications gained abroad. This 'cold pogrom' aimed to compel Jews to emigrate; but many frontiers were closing to them and in 1937 only nine thousand were able to emigrate from Poland. By 1939 possibly one third of the three million Jews in Poland depended largely on relief from private Jewish organizations financed from America.

The reactionary National Democrats scorned the Government's policy as too tame. Their main party organ, *Warszawski Dziennik Narodowy* (20 November 1938), insisted: 'It is not

9

enough to show the Jews the door; one should push them through by means of a "surgical operation" which would deprive them legally of livelihood in Poland.' In January 1939 a proposal came before the Sejm (Parliament) for a law which would deprive most Jews of civil and political rights: the right to vote, to be an official, to practise some of the professions, particularly law and medicine, or to own property. Jewish emigration was to be helped by a special fund raised by forced contributions from Jewish organizations and wealthy Jews. The Jews took the brunt of the country's social and economic chaos. At the League of Nations Poland asked for measures to remove Jews from the country at the rate of 100,000 a year.

It is against this discreditable background that the occasional anti-semitic writings to be found in the publications from Niepokalanów must be judged.

'Spodek' spoke too of the criticisms of Kolbe's papers as naive in content. When they were first published there was much ignorance and illiteracy, particularly in the countryside. Kolbe was concerned to address the peasants of his day. The language was simple and direct – even those who could not read could profit from pictures – and the papers strove to help people with their daily problems. Other journals on a higher plane were published for special groups such as clergy and students. Since the war the people have become more literate, knowledgeable and spiritually more mature.

Before the war 'Spodek' said that Kolbe was known to the general public not because of his spirituality but as a man with a position, Guardian of Niepokalanów. Now he is admired throughout Poland – his image is different from that of other Catholic saints because he is a man of our own time. Many heroes of the Church are separated from us by centuries but he is one of us, our living generation, persecuted during the war. He came to be seen as the symbol of suffering in the camps and all those who had lost family and friends could identify with his victorious act which upheld human and universal values. 'Spodek' added that there was much discussion in Poland after the war about Kolbe's activities and the circumstances of his death at Auschwitz. He urged me to read a controversial article by Jan Józef Szczepański, published in the literary monthly *Twórczość* (Creativity) April 1974. Szczepański is a well known author and a former chairman of the Polish Union of Writers. The Union has been suspended by the military régime which assumed control in Poland on 13 December 1981. *Twórczość* was also suspended by the junta. Szczepański argues that Kolbe was wary of intellectualism, for he felt that to rely on your own intellect was contrary to humility, the hallmark of a good Christian. This is why out of all the ways of practising religion Kolbe chose the most traditional and emotional way, the Marian cult which still characterizes Polish Christianity and is etched deep in the nation's history.

Poland's holy shrine Jasna Góra, Częstochowa, is still the home of the Black Madonna, a painting many ascribe to St Luke, which was placed there six hundred years ago. At times of crisis the sanctuary has served as an inspiration to revive patriotism. In Polish tradition there has long been the fusion of the Marian cult with the self-preservation of Poland; the idea of the Militia was born from the same tradition – Polonus defensor Mariae – a Pole defender of the Virgin Mary.

My visit to Auschwitz hovered over me like a black bird. I dreaded to find commercialism, or sensation-seekers looking to satisfy macabre appetites. It is not like that. The barracks are now a museum of remembrance for the dead of many nations. It is a shrine and tourists come reverently as pilgrims. Many weep for the piteousness of it all. I reproached myself for not taking flowers. I did not sleep the night before, nor the following night, when the mind defroze and the full horror of the atrocious place filled my soul, a place where deeds of such inhumanity had been committed that forgiveness seemed impossible. Yet I had already met a man of sufficient charity the previous summer, a man who had survived eight concentration camps and could not bring himself to hate the Germans. Dr Jósef Garliński is now president of the Union of

Polish Writers Abroad and one of his books, *Fighting Ausch-witz*, offered as a memorial to those who perished, tells the story of the camp's underground movement. He said that the young SS men had been brain-washed, trained to be brutal. 'They could have been your sons or mine', he told me. 'Every-thing was against the man who was kind-hearted: his orders, his colleagues, his superiors. If he showed any kindness, he was considered to be soft, a bad German and a bad soldier. He had to be much above the common lot to behave his own way.' Yet Dr Garliński devotes a chapter in his book to 'good Germans'.

The journey to Auschwitz – how the Poles hate that Ger-man name for Oświęcim – was made alone for my interpreter had begged to be excused; her private grief over loved ones who were taken away was too great. So I booked overnight at a Cracow hotel and engaged a taxi to take me to the camp and back, some fifty kilometres each way. Through an intro-duction to the Polish Pen Club, *Związek Literatów Polskich*, my personal guide was to meet me at the gates.

It was a honey-coloured May morning as we drove through copses and curving lanes. Countrywomen in long skirts and high boots were on their knees in the fields sowing and hoeing. I saw one old woman trudging along the road driving a solitary cow before her. Many acres of land were untended and wild flowers romped everywhere. The countryside was soft and protective, as if wanting to shelter us from the harsh enormity of the camp we would soon encounter.

My guide, a man of spare build with a thin sensitive face, spoke excellent English. He was a chemical engineer who guided visitors as a part-time job. For months he had to take tranquillizers so that he could master his emotions to concen-trate on the facts. He saw the job as all-important. 'People must know the truth, they have a duty to remember.' There was still much ignorance and ingenuousness; one American woman thought the camp had been built as a film-set. He explained the difference between the extermination camp where victims were murdered straight from the goods trains and the work camp where prisoners worked themselves to death – of 400,000 only 60,000 survived the labour kommandos. Small children were judged useless and destroyed. All children were made to walk under a wire; if their heads touched they had proved themselves big enough for work and so were spared. Word of this cruel aptitude test was whispered to new arrivals and mothers would frantically coax their children 'to walk tall', tiptoe.

I could not comprehend the cynical 'charades' of the Nazis: numerous Jewish tailoresses were given special permits in Czech and German for 'resettlement'; and those going into the 'ablutions' were told to remember where they laid their clothes so that they might find them again after bathing. There were careful records of young people who were alleged to have died from twenty-five different diseases including such 'natural causes' as heart attacks.

I was shown the barracks where prisoners, soon to be plagued by epidemics and attacked by rats, slept on dirty straw in stalls like cattle. I stood in the place where over the years 20,000 men had been shot in the neck facing a black wall. I saw the convalescent block which my guide called 'the waiting-room' for the crematoria because if you were ill you were worthless. I saw the block where medical experiments were carried out to turn people into zombies to be exploited for German labour; the results were horrendous; gangrene set in and many went mad. I looked with incredulous pity at the gallery of photographs: each prisoner had his or her picture taken from three angles; my guide commented shortly, 'But their appearance soon changed in the camp.' A gentle well-mannered man, he was unrelentingly thorough. In a numbed state I followed him through the gas chambers where two thousand prisoners at a time were eliminated – you can still smell the gas – and on to the cremation ovens. Human ashes became fertilizer.

But for me tears came when I saw personal belongings: the suitcases so carefully labelled, toothbrushes, shaving brushes, hair brushes, glasses, a pyramid of children's shoes. And toys.

There was a ton or two of human hair shown – tons more had lined the suits of German officers.

We went finally to Cell 18 of Block 11 where Maksymilian died. Here Pope John Paul II lit a candle upon his homecoming in 1979. There were a million pilgrims at the outdoor Mass and the Pope was assisted by former prisoners who were priests. Special pennants had been made for the pilgrims and my guide gave me one. Made of fabric in the blue and white colours of the Madonna it carries on one side a red triangle with a P, and Kolbe's prison number 16670 underneath, and on the reverse is printed Oświęcim, 7.6.1979.

The Pope made a speech which moved and challenged the huge congregation. His words remembered by my guide were simply these, '. . . in this place Maksymilian Kolbe won a spiritual victory like that of Christ himself.'

That same afternoon Tadek, my taxi-driver, drove me to see Professor Rząsa's sculptures in the modern and mighty church at Nowa Huta (New Foundry). When the new town was planned for workers at the mammoth Lenin steel plant, there was no provision for places of worship because the government reasoned that nearby Cracow had plenty of churches, but the people of Nowa Huta wanted their own as the focus of their lives. There were minor riots over government opposition and men marched in the streets in protest. Eventually the government relented and in 1967 issued a permit to build a church. Ten years later, before a crowd of fifty thousand, the present Pope, then Karol Wojtyła, Archbishop of Cracow, laid the foundation stone which came from the grave of St Peter in Rome and was given to Poland by Pope Paul VI. Tadek knew about the sculptures – there is also a steel sculpture of Christ which captures both the agony and the glory – and insisted upon coming into the church with me. We found the one of Father Kolbe, wearing prison clothes, in the Chapel of Forgiveness on the lower level. It is a dramatic work which eschews the emotional religiosity which attaches to many saints and shows modern man in the

14

thraldom of twentieth-century calvary. The chapel remembers Poland's Occupation (1939–45) and Kolbe represents the tragedy of the Polish people. The Madonna is made from steel splinters removed from dead soldiers after the battle of Monte Cassino.

The architect of the church was Wojciech Pietrzyk, whose design aims to express the symbolism of the arch as 'The Hope of the Earth'. A hymn of praise in concrete and stone, it soars exultantly to its climax, a roof shaped like a massive ark. One side of the church is covered with two million granite pebbles collected from riverbeds all over the country. You do not 'visit' this church, but forget the world outside for a moment in prayer. It seemed natural for us to kneel together – a Polish taxi-driver from Cracow and an English woman writer from a west country village – and say a little prayer.

Tadek then took me to the railway station and bought my ticket. We had arranged a price in advance for the day. He refused a tip and waited to see me on to the train for Warsaw. He had done far more than was expected of him and now he stood waving goodbye like a close relative.

The unquenchable spirit of Poland lives on, for surviving is the Polish profession. Silent witnesses to their suffering are the simple shrines in every square and around every street corner in the capital where three-quarters of a million died in the last war. Such memorials are adopted by schools and organizations in the city which lay fresh flowers, and once again it hurt me that I had not taken roses to Auschwitz where Maksymilian's deed had brought a universal message of hope for the Church and the world, symbolizing the banishment of hate through love. Kolbe died a lonely and seemingly anonymous death. He could not rely on the subject of his sacrifice living to talk about it, and the identity of that man was immaterial; a stranger, he could have been an atheist, heretic, Jew or Freemason.

I met Franciszek Gajowniczek and his wife, Helena, in their modest home in Brzeg on the Odra river. He was then in his eighty-first year and his wife four years younger. I found an erect, soldierly man with a strong authoritative face and, surprisingly, merry eyes. Helena has a kind and lined face which tells of a mother's sorrow. Both young sons died on the streets, killed by Russian shells before their father could be reunited with them. Helena became a chain-smoker from that day. Did Franciszek experience any sense of guilt that his life should be spared for that of such a holy man? Did he feel a burden of stewardship, pressure to live his life in a special way because of what had happened? How has he seen his role over the past forty years? He has thought deeply about the extraordinary events which befell him. He spoke frankly and later I will reveal his feelings and conclusions. Sufficient here to record that he spends much of his time as a missioner of the Church, spreading the ideals of Father Kolbe.

So Maksymilian's life continues as an allegory and source of strength for persecution appears unending. His victory should be known not only to those who profess faith but to all who applaud courage.

Maksymilian Kolbe belonged to the Franciscan Order of Friars Minor (Conventual) whose Rule teaches the brothers to remain lowly. They are called minors because they do not dream of becoming majors. The new saint has innocently and gloriously transgressed that Rule. I offer this book as a salute to sacrifice and in joy to mark the canonization.

CHAPTER TWO

It was clear to everyone in the Kolbe household that Rajmund was not his customary cheerful and energetic self; he was unnaturally quiet and often looked red-eyed. His parents worried lest he were ill but he had no fever, complained of no pains.

In the parlour of the timbered cottage was an altar, contrived between two cupboards, with a picture of Our Lady of Częstochowa, the holy painting of the Black Madonna depicting Mary in strong angular lines. This simple shrine, lit by oil lamps, was used by the family and their neighbours. Marianna became aware that her small son was retreating there more often and for longer periods, and sometimes it was easy to see that he had been crying. It was around the time of his first communion and he was ten years old. Eventually she could bear his sadness no longer, and drawing the child to her, implored him, 'Come, you must tell everything to your mother.' Her manner was gentle, but her voice had a characteristic firmness which made her plea a command. With tears in his eyes Rajmund reminded his mother of her own words when after some boyish escapade she had reproved him saying, 'Whatever kind of a man will you grow up to be?' Rajmund had taken her admonition to heart and become sad and silent. He went to pray before the altar of the Virgin Mary in the parish church and asked the Holy Mother to tell him what kind of a man he would become. At once Mary appeared before him, holding two crowns, one white, the other red. She told him the white crown was for purity, the red for martyrdom. With love in her face she looked at him and asked which he would choose. 'I will take both', he said.

17

Mary gazed at him as tenderly as any mother and disappeared.

The momentous secret was shared. What had been in Rajmund's mind as he lay in bed through the silent hours, trembling and exultant? The thought of a future abundant with hope and adventure which beckoned now with such awesome certainty to a boy of ten? The daunting prospect of untold suffering or the promise of glory? Maybe he rubbed his eyes and told himself it was but a day-dream, that to-morrow he would laugh again and play with his friends in the carelessness of childhood, the long and beautiful years. Whatever his lonely thoughts had been, the boy became composed, happy again; but serious beyond his age. He had put away childish things; that part of his life had ended abruptly. Turning to his mother, he said in a matter-of-fact voice which made his words the more extraordinary, 'Now when I go to church with my father and mother, it is not my parents but Joseph and Mary.' His mother kept the secret of the two crowns until after her son's death, but naturally enough she told a neighbour about the vision. Her whispered words came in a rush like a small wind. 'Holy Mother appeared to Mundzio' – as she called Rajmund fondly – 'in the church.' She added mysteriously, 'She showed him some symbols.' Marianna refused to say more.

For Marianna it was like Simeon's prophecy to Mary, mother of Jesus. She prepared herself for her beloved son to die a martyr with feelings both of an almost incredulous joy and the bitter sorrow of a loving mother. Like Mary she knew a sword would pierce her own soul too.

*   *   *

The family lived in Zduńska Wola, a poor town near Lódź, the second largest city in Poland and centre of the textile industry, the Polish Manchester. Rajmund was the second son in a family of five boys, born on 8 January 1894 to Juliusz and Marianna Kolbe, and baptized the same day; his elder

18

brother, Franciszek, was also born in Zduńsha Wola seventeen months earlier.

The parents were devout Catholics and took careful thought for the boys' state of grace as well as their physical well-being. On Sundays and Feast Days the whole family went to church: mother, a short dumpy figure in a black coat and carrying a big prayer-book, her ebony hair plaited and piled in a bun under a black handkerchief; and father, tall, blonde and good-looking, proud of the well-scrubbed children. Most years, even when times were hard, Juliusz made a pilgrimage of a hundred kilometres to Częstochowa, where the painting of the Black Madonna is enshrined at the sanctuary on Jasna Góra, the Bright Mountain. Marianna carried out her moral duties to her sons with scrupulous concern and required much of them in obedience, punctuality and helpfulness in the home. She showed an intense and serious nature although one neighbour records she was 'ever-smiling'. Juliusz is likely to have spared more time of the little leisure any of them had left from the hard demands of scraping a living, to playing with the boys. He hoped to see them grow lithe and strong and he would invent games with his characteristic enthusiasm. When snow fell he would challenge them to barefoot races in the fields.

Juliusz Kolbe's parents were also ardent Catholics who worked as weavers as well as running a small farm at Zduńska Wola. While their other sons had to serve for a time in the army, Juliusz, as the eldest of the four children, was exempt. His family was probably better off than his future in-laws, the Dąbrowscy – a typical Polish name – who lived nearby.

Marianna Dąbrowska was a modest girl and deeply religious; it was her practice to say a whole rosary every day. But she was frustrated in her dearest wish to become a nun because Russia, since 1815, had controlled much of the country and periodically suppressed the convents, driving many sisters 'underground' to work secretly in the disguise of ordinary dress. Marianna was taught by her parents and worked as a child in a weaving workshop at home. Her sister, Anna Kubiak, recounted how hard they all worked. After collecting the wool from the Jewish factory-owners their looms were busy from early morning until late at night and it seemed to Anna that when they returned the beautiful fabrics her parents feared the Jews might find fault with their work, and so they went nervously as if to a court of law.

Juliusz and Marianna met in worship at church. When they married they made their first home in Zduńska Wola. Juliusz was by nature an entrepreneur, showing both initiative and inventiveness; an open, brave and cheerful man he made friends easily. While Marianna occupied herself with the babies and the housework, he ran a workshop at home. He was kind to his pupils and workers although like all cottage weavers they were miserably paid and had to toil long hours to make ends meet. Juliusz Kolbe's weavers spun from 6.00 a.m. to 8.00 p.m. for six days a week, while Juliusz himself spent much time negotiating business with the Jews. There was a large Jewish community in Lódź and environs for it was the Jews and the Germans who controlled the home-weaving industry.

Juliusz always felt a Pole although his name originated from the Czech. In the first centuries after Christ the forebears of the Czechs settled in Bohemia – now part of the republic of Czechoslovakia – and during the Middle Ages Germans came to live on the slopes separating Bohemia from Germany. By the days of the Habsburgs, the powerful Austrian imperial family, these German settlers had become so prosperous through mining that they dominated the ruling classes. Czech was no longer spoken except by the peasants and was not studied in the schools. German had become the almost universal language of the kingdom. In 1526 Bohemia was annexed by the Austrian Empire, and it was under the dominance of Austria that the native Czech name of Kolber or Korbirz was Germanized to Kolbe.

Juliusz' grandfather, Paul, was born in Stoky in south-east

Bohemia, and when he emigrated to Poland with a group of unemployed Czechs to look for work in the 1840s he brought the name of Kolbe to Poland. It was the dawn of the textile industry and new centres of woollen manufacture around Lódź, Pabianice and Zduńska Wola offered some sort of livelihood to these poor emigrants.

In 1895 Juliusz and Marianna Kolbe reluctantly moved from Zduńska Wola to nearby Lódź because Poland itself was now in the thrall of a depression and conditions for the peasants were harsh. Their boys were then one and two years old and it was here that their third son, Józef, was born. Juliusz was compelled to find work in a factory; a natural leader, he found it difficult to be a workman. Marianna did nothing to soothe his restlessness because she too was uneasy; she feared the temptations of a teeming big town for the growing sons, for when the first factories were built Lódź mushroomed into a chaos of tenement houses. Neither parent craved wealth; in fact, Marianna in her simple and pious mind saw danger in riches; money was a hazard on the way to perfection. They both wanted a peaceful, more rural environment in which to nurture their children. So a year later they moved to Jutrzkowice, a village near Pabianice on the outskirts of the drab Lódź complex, where they had a weaving workshop once more in their own cottage, and a plot of land to cultivate. They made yet another move to a larger house in Pabianice when their family increased. Sadly both their fourth and fifth sons died in early childhood: Walenty was born in 1897 and died a year later; Antoni was born in 1901 and died when he was four.

In 1904–5 there were strikes in Lódź and all over the country and the entire population demonstrated its fervent wish for social justice and self-government. All the conditions were ripe for rebellion: the peasantry was impoverished, the factory workers intoxicated by Marxism, Siberian exiles embittered, and the oppressed nationalities resentful – even schoolchildren and their teachers went on strike demanding Polish as the language of education. In clashes with police and Cossacks hundreds of workers were killed, wounded and arrested. The clergy of the Russian dominions were asked by the Archbishop of Warsaw to use their influence to calm the turmoil.

The victories of the Japanese fighting Russia in 1904–5 meant loss of face for the Tsarist Empire, and the Poles saw a chance of liberating Russian Poland by a rebellion under more favourable circumstances than previous risings. Anticipating riots on May Day 1905, thirty-five thousand people applied for passports to leave the country.

By early October troubles had erupted in Russia. The printers of Moscow had struck and their example encouraged other trades to come out. Towards the end of the month a railway strike set in motion a general strike in Russia, and the Poles reacted with a strike in Warsaw which spread rapidly. Tsar Nicholas II was forced to issue the manifesto of 17–30 October 1905 promising Russia a legislative parliament. Thus the Russian autocracy made a pact with the rebels in their Empire, including the Poles. They granted a constitution, proclaiming an elected parliament or duma, which gave small voice to the peasantry. It was but a sop to the Poles; and they were to remain under strict Russian rule until the First World War.

The Polish leaders of this revolution attacked the Church because it was widely believed that priests were backing the rapacious capitalists. Many workers stopped going to Mass. The Kolbes stayed loyal and persevered in the education of their sons in the ways of the faith. Juliusz and Marianna were conscientious Catholics; and both belonged to the Third Order of St Francis. Originally known by the name The Order of Penitence, St Francis founded a strong arm of auxiliaries for lay men and women, who, while remaining in the world, radiate the Franciscan spirit outside the cloister and perform works of piety. St Francis started the Third Order for he knew that although his followers were legion few could adopt the austere life of the religious.

Ironically, in the light of Rajmund's vision, it was their

eldest son, Franciszek, whom the parents decided would take the cloth and for whom they were willing to make financial sacrifices. Neighbours remarked that while they always acknowledged Rajmund to be a 'good boy', it was his brother who appeared to be the favourite. Juliusz taught the boys to read and write, but as he had had only an elementary education himself he paid for Franciszek to attend business school in Pabianice. There were no free schools under Russian occupation although the need was clamorous; the census of 1897 had revealed that only thirty per cent of the people in Russian Poland could read and write. The family budget was squeezed and the Kolbes turned their talents to running a small shop in the straggling suburbs to serve the workers in a nearby factory. Juliusz obtained goods on credit and was obliged to pay usurious interest, but the workers also bought on credit and paid no interest, so this venture did not flourish. To help out, Marianna worked as midwife in the neighbourhood, acting on commonsense rather than any formal training. There was much ignorance and superstition associated with childbirth, particularly in the villages. Doctors basted newborn babies with red wine as an antiseptic. Marianna Kolbe must have been a very present source of strength, but it is doubtful whether she did much to augment the family's income because she waived payment if her patients were poor, and most were. There was humiliating poverty and on Sundays the peasants, who were both religious and ritualistic, would often walk to church in regional dress holding their shoes in their hands to save wear.

Rajmund, who had a gift for arithmetic, helped in the shop and liked to surprise his 'dear Mamma' when she came home tired after delivering a baby. Such surprises were meals he made out of meagre ingredients but plentiful imagination. Rajmund also had a facility for Latin. The local priest, Father Jankowski, had given the boys some preliminary instruction and their father learnt with them. A neighbour recollects, 'However often I came to visit him, he was always learning Latin!' Now Rajmund impressed the local chemist, Mr Kotowski, to excellent effect. He presented a prescription for one of his mother's nursing cases asking for the medicine by its Latin name. Mr Kotowski discovered the lad was not attending school and offered to tutor him. Rajmund went home as if on wings. Soon he was abreast of Franciszek and convinced his parents they could no longer afford to neglect his education and he joined his brother in the second class at Pabianice.

They were diligent boys at school where there was a high standard of tuition. Until 1905 the teaching was in Russian: school pupils could learn little about Polish history and literature and had to recite praises to the Russian leaders. There was, however, a secret organization to provide patriotic books, and 'underground' universities were served by the best professors. After the 1905 strike all subjects were taught in Polish. The school day was long, eight to four, and there were 'extras' like singing for Franciszek and Rajmund who belonged to the choir at the parish church. Rajmund made many friends whom he helped with their homework, particularly in maths and physics.

The Kolbe boys had a strict, even rigid, upbringing, but their parents brought their own compensating qualities to the task. Mrs Kolbe probably had the stronger influence because she was single-minded; in her old-fashioned light she saw her duty as guarding her children against immorality. She was so strict that the boys were not allowed even to speak to girls without specific reason. It is not in the nature of boys – even saints in the making – to be angels, and accounts vary of how she punished them for everyday naughtiness. One neighbour mentions chastisement with a strap; another declares that physical punishment was never used. It is on record that they were frightened of mother when they came home late from play. Despite the very different personalities of their parents there were no quarrels in the home. Mr Kolbe brimmed with ideas. He was one of a group of friends who met frequently to read and discuss; and they had their own communal library. As well as a booklover, Juliusz was a practical man, always inventing and experimenting. He raised money for the

24

Church and helped others. The inheritance of the Kolbe sons was rich because it fired all three boys to seek something more than a quiet life.

In the Polish provinces annexed by Austria in the First Partition (1772) and in the Third Partition (1795) the rulers respected the religion of their subjects and most novitiates and seminaries for religious orders were in that zone. Missionaries often made secret sorties to the more repressive territories of Russian Poland to recruit. In such a way Franciszek and Rajmund Kolbe were canvassed. As schoolboys they attended a retreat by the Franciscan Provincial, Father Peregrine Hazsela, who was looking for candidates for the Franciscan minor seminary at the ancient and faithful city of Lwów. Both boys asked to go and their parents approved. At the beginning of the term in 1907 Juliusz went with his sons to Cracow, crossing the Russian-Austrian frontier secretly as the Poles often did. Here he bade them godspeed and the boys took the train to Lwów. Rajmund amazed his teachers at the minor seminary with his grasp of mathematics and the sciences, and his originality of mind. Fascinated by the challenge of space, he began to design machines to put men on the moon. He also developed an interest in military stratagems and war games, and began to argue to himself that he could surely best serve God in the world as engineer, inventor, or soldier rather than as a friar who must vow to obey, even those of lesser intelligence. Obedience he knew was the law of the soldier too; but he planned to give the orders.

When sixteen, he needed to decide if he would enter the novitiate to become a Franciscan friar. He resolved to tell the Minister Provincial that he had been mistaken in his vocation; he would use his intelligence to win victories for God on the battlefield as a soldier. Like Francis of Assisi he was deluded about the nature of such armed conquests. Francis dreamed of being a knight errant and the glory which he desired was to be won by daring exploits in the field, but on an expedition into Apulia he was not far from Assisi when a voice ordered him, 'Return to the land where you were born, for through me your vision of arms shall be realized in the spirit.'

It was a providential visit from his mother which deterred Rajmund from his eager decision to become a soldier. She called at the friary which ran the minor seminary with the news that his younger brother, Józef, had also elected to become a religious. Both parents saw their parental duties happily fulfilled: now they had decided to follow their hearts' desire; she was joining the Benedictine Sisters at Lwów and Juliusz the Franciscans at Cracow. 'All the family will work for God,' she said joyously. Putting aside his dream of a resplendent uniform Rajmund asked the Minister Provincial for the simple Franciscan habit. His new religious name was Maksymilian, after Maximilian, a young citizen of the Roman Empire executed at the age of twenty-one for his refusal to serve as a soldier. Roman law obliged a son to follow his father's profession, and Maximilian, as a soldier's son, was brought before Dio Cassius, proconsul in North Africa, on 12 March 295. A contemporary record of the trial, which was probably held in Carthage, records that Maximilian told the proconsul, 'I will not be a soldier of this world for I am a soldier of Christ. My army is of the army of God.' Dio Cassius argued, 'There are Christian soldiers serving our rulers', to which the young man retorted with spirit, 'That is their business. I also am a Christian and I cannot serve.' The proconsul pressed him, 'But what harm do soldiers do?' Maximilian replied curtly, 'You know well enough.' Dio Cassius gave no quarter: 'I shall condemn you to death for contempt of the Army. Your impiety makes you refuse military service and you shall be punished as a warning to others.'

After he had been accepted by the Provincial as a candidate, Rajmund made a retreat. For two weeks he kept his lay clothes but led the same life as a novice, and in the quietude of his cell he meditated upon the steadfastness of the brother-

26

hood and the adventures awaiting him once armoured as a knight of Christ.

The Primitive Rule which Francis wrote was short, composed of the very words of the holy Gospel, to which he had added a few prescriptions necessary for a holy life in common. Pope Innocent III assented to this fantastic design with these words, 'Go in peace . . . And when the Almighty has multiplied you and given you new grace, return and make me a sharer in your joy.' St Francis wrote two subsequent Rules without fundamental differences. The first of these two Rules, written in 1221, was approved by Pope Honorius III, who two years later accepted the second Rule which is still today the official constitution of the Order of Friars Minor. This is how the Rule describes the life of the brothers: 'to observe the Holy Gospel of Jesus Christ by living in obedience, without property and in chastity.'

On Friday 4 September 1910 after the conventual Mass, Rajmund knelt before the altar in the ancient ceremony to enter the novitiate. Firstly, the Provincial relieved Rajmund of his lay jacket, saying in Latin, 'May the Lord deliver you from the old man and his actions.' Vesting him with the habit he prayed, 'May the Lord clothe you with the new man created in justice and the holiness of truth.' Next he put on the capuche with the words, 'May the Lord place upon your head the helmet of salvation, to make you invincible against the attacks of the devil.' The young friar took the cord to encircle the habit and the celebrant prayed again, 'Gird him also, O Lord, with the girdle of purity to stifle in his body the ardour of the passions and preserve him in the virtues of continence and chastity.' Lastly the Provincial handed Rajmund a candle, 'Receive my dear brother, the light of Christ as a token of your immortality, so that dead to the world you may live henceforth for God.' With a touch on the arm, he exhorted him, 'Arise from the dead and Christ will enlighten you.' Then came a concluding prayer and the invocation, 'Veni Creator Spiritus.' The Provincial now addressed him upon leaving by his new name in religion: 'My son, in future you will not be known as Rajmund but as Friar Maksymilian.'

Friar Maksymilian accepted his habit as a uniform and the candle as a sword. The words of the celebrant made clear the enemy. All the brothers passed before him and gave him the kiss of peace in welcome to the Franciscan family.

After a year's probation in the novitiate, in which he fought many a spiritual battle when assailed by doubt, on 5 September 1911 he took his temporary vows, binding for three years, and after finishing middle school was sent to Cracow to study philosophy. Maksymilian was now used to the rigours of obedience, poverty, cold and hunger, and although some of the other brothers at the Franciscan friary grumbled about their tasks, he would saw the wood and clean the pots and pans with the greatest joy. He was humble and shy and behaved as one who was given something beyond material value.

Marianna Kolbe stayed three years with the Benedictine Sisters at Lwów, to be near her young sons, before coming to Cracow in 1913 to join the Felician Sisters in the quiet tree-shaded street, ul Smoleńsk.

Long before the thrushes began to chirrup in the walled gardens of the convent, Marianna had risen from her hard bed and was singing religious songs. This was nothing unusual for she was uncompromising in self-discipline. She chose to sleep on a wooden plank and every morning rose at four o'clock, an hour before holy Mass, to allow more time for prayer and song. She had a low mellifluous voice and the sisters often gathered to listen outside her small austere room, number 234, on the ground floor of the massive house.

After breakfast Marianna would arrange her day. She acted as *odźwierna*, keeper of the gate, and carried out all the worldly business of the convent which was an enclosed Order. Many of her duties took her into the town; to pay for the water, collect medicines, and give orders to the tradespeople. To carry out such errands she would put on her big black coat and hat for she always dressed in black. She was mindful to keep on good terms with the butcher: for his part she was one of his best customers because there were a hundred sisters at the convent and he respected her thriftiness and house-wifely good sense. Sometimes the shopkeepers would present her with little gifts on account of the quantities she bought and these she would bestow upon the Franciscan fathers whom she knew were in need. She found satisfaction in the sameness of her days, and the orderliness of the convent appealed to her methodical disposition. As well as the marketing she helped with the housework and made time for charitable work among the poor.

Marianna was over forty and described in those days as 'elderly' when she joined the Felician Sisters. As a married woman she could not be accepted as a nun, but only as a lay sister. This was to be her home for the next thirty-three years, and she found an oasis of peace behind the black gates of the convent. The thick walls of the old house embraced her like strong arms. She was like a mother and took care of everything.

Juliusz was as great a patriot as he was a loyal Catholic, and saw no contradiction in giving his fealty to both country and faith. His volatile nature looked for challenge to stretch mind and muscle and, unlike his wife Marianna, who found purpose and repose with the nuns, he soon realized he was not attuned to life in a friary. At the parting from his family in 1910 he joined the Franciscan fathers at Cracow and then went to Lwów where the friary owned gardens and farmland. Here he helped the gardener and his habitual cheerfulness soon won him the friendship of the young seminarians to whom he smuggled fruit. Next he worked on the farm and was able to introduce many improvements. Not all his ideas were appreciated. It appears he irritated the administrator, Brother Roch, by giving names to the cows and displaying them on plaques above their heads in the cow-stalls; Brother Roch did not like such novelties.

Juliusz felt trapped by the routine of the good fathers, which went unruffled by new excitements. His natural impulse drove him to seek fresh outlets for his energies and he left for Częstochowa, the Lourdes of Poland, where he found more time to pray, and to plan. He opened a new bookshop there; it was at once popular and it soon brought good profits which Juliusz gave gladly to religious and patriotic movements. But not all its customers seemed the kind of people usually to be found browsing among the shelves of booksellers. Behind the innocent facade of the bookshop he distributed 'underground' newspapers and recruited men to fight on the Russian Front.

His hero was Józef Piłsudski, a great soldier without formal military training, who was to become head of the new Polish State in November 1918. He was a vital man with a black walrus moustache whose charisma and passion for independence won him wide appeal among the patriotic Poles. It was probably his dash and daring that won the allegiance of Juliusz Kolbe, himself a man of action. For a staunch Roman Catholic, his attachment to Piłsudski was remarkable because many of the more radical Piłsudski supporters were strongly anticlerical, and the Church had forged close links with the National Democrats, Piłsudski's bitterest opponents. Nor could it have helped Piłsudski's image with fellow Catholics that in 1899 he married in a Protestant church the divorced wife of a Polish civil engineer in Russian service. She was Maria Juszkiewicz, famous for her beauty and audacity for she used to carry illegal literature under her clothing – up to four stones of 'underground' newspapers. It is strange that Piłsudski was not punished by the Church because he married a divorcee. When she died in 1921 he married again that same year. His second wife, Aleksandra Szczerbińska, was also a resolute worker for the independence movement. This time the ceremony was attended with Catholic rites. Piłsudski was not zealous in his religious observance but he continued to regard himself a Catholic and carried a medallion of the Virgin Mary all his life.

The second son of an impecunious Polish noble, his mother had filled him with hate for the imperial regime of the Tsars. As a hot-head of twenty he was arrested on a charge of plotting to assassinate the Tsar, Alexander III, and banished to eastern Siberia for five years – the same conspiracy for which Lenin's brother was hanged.

When Piłsudski returned to Poland in 1892 he joined the newly formed Polish Socialist Party (PPS) and soon became its leader, producing a clandestine newspaper, the *Robotnik* (The Worker). The Party suffered a severe setback, however, when in February 1900 the secret press for the paper was discovered in the Piłsudski flat above a haberdasher's in Lódź, and Piłsudski was imprisoned in the Warsaw Citadel. Here he feigned madness so convincingly that he was transferred to a military hospital in St Petersburg from which he escaped in May 1901. At first he took refuge in Cracow but a year later he was back in Russian Poland looking after the party organization.

His rival, Roman Dmowski, founder of the National Democrats, was Piłsudski's opposite, in background, personality and politics. He came from humble origins – his father was a roofer – and he was a cautious statesman without Piłsudski's fire. Dmowski named Germany as Poland's chief enemy, believing that German ambitions in Eastern Europe would lead to a clash with Russia. He hoped to engage the trust of the Russian government with his anti-German policies so that Russia might reach some agreement with the Poles. Piłsudski mistrusted Russia and believed co-operation with Austria to be Poland's best hope to win civil rights – tactics which were to let him down in November 1916.

In the 1905 revolution the National Democrats first became important in Polish political life when they opposed the attempts of the PPS under Piłsudski to organize the national insurrection. But Piłsudski took control of the fighting organization of the party and was able to lead terrorist attacks on Russian government outposts.

Foreseeing a European war, Piłsudski was now convinced

it was imperative to organize Polish legions of trained soldiers and in 1908 he formed the Union of Active Struggle with money stolen from a Russian mail train by an armed band which he led himself. Two years later he converted his organization into a legal Union of Riflemen. At a meeting in Paris in 1914 when war was imminent, he told supporters, 'The independence of Poland will only be achieved if Russia is beaten by Austria-Hungary and Germany, and Germany vanquished by France, Great Britain and the United States; it is our duty to bring that about.'

Until 1916 Piłsudski's legionaries fought under the Austria-Hungary command, at least technically. But his co-operation with the Austrians was to be short-lived. On 5 November 1916 Germany and Austria-Hungary proclaimed the independence of Poland. They were starved of manpower and now hoped that Polish divisions would man the eastern front and so free German divisions to fight on the west. Piłsudski was prepared to accept the command of the new Polish Army but he demanded as his price the creation of a genuine Polish civilian government. When he realized the Germans were interested only in a puppet state he refused to take the military oath of allegiance to the Reich which they insisted upon, and most of his supporters followed his example. In July 1917 he was arrested and interned in Magdeburg Fortress in east Germany.

Franciszek Kolbe, the eldest son, gained leave of absence from the Franciscan Order at the outbreak of war, and joined Piłsudski's Legions. He was wounded in battle many times. His father Juliusz had been one of the first to enlist as a legionary and persuaded many men to follow him into the ranks. When war came his unit left Cracow to go eastwards. Juliusz was wounded early on in fighting with the Russians and taken prisoner. Many of his comrades-in-arms had Austrian passports: his was Russian and as a Russian subject he had no rights as a prisoner-of-war. He was hanged as a traitor near Olkusz in 1914. He was 43 years old.

His death brought much grief to the family, especially to his sons whose childhood ties had been strong; they remembered him as a cheerful affectionate father who always made time for games; a man with a strong impulse for adventure, who had bestowed upon them many gifts, notably a love of life and its abundant promise. When Maksymilian heard the news he was a long way from home for in the winter of 1912 he had been sent with six confrères to Rome. The Franciscan Superiors believed the experience would broaden the provincialism of the young Poles.

CHAPTER THREE

Maksymilian was exhilarated and inspired by the city of Rome and in letters to his mother he wrote with wonderment about the international flavour of the Franciscan College. 'Among the friars are Germans, Hungarians, Poles, Czechs, Yugoslavs, Maltese and many Italians . . . Rome is one enormous reliquary with the bones and blood of saints and at the same time monuments to famous Emperors.' The friars were fortunate for the college in Via San Teodoro was at the foot of one of the most romantic hills of Rome – the Palatine, where marble ruins can be seen amidst a sweet wilderness of fern and wild flowers.

On her festival, the brothers attended Solemn Vespers at the church of St Cecilia, formerly a palace where the saint, the patroness of church music, was martyred. Maksymilian wrote, 'It was an enormous experience – beautiful choir (our choirs could not equal it), a hundred chandeliers, the church full of clerics from all over the world.'

In another letter he described the students' first audience with Pope Pius X. 'From early morning there was great excitement at the College. We were all dressed as for a Feast in our best habits. I climbed the marble steps at the Vatican with joy and emotion. The Pope not only gave us a general Blessing but allowed each of us to kiss the Papal ring. I thought, "Here is Peter in the presence of his successor – how big and holy is our Catholic Church but why is it that not everyone knows Christ and his Mother."' He longed to be an apostle and spread the word of God.

Rome stirred the soul and fed the intellect, but it was at this summit of excitement that Maksymilian was first stricken

34

by serious illness. When he arrived he had rosy cheeks, perpetually cold hands and chilblains, so his Superior sent him for medical advice. Such symptoms suggested troubles with circulation. He also had violent headaches which may have been caused by nervous tension for he was nervous by nature. His hands were often trembling, his fingers drumming. Yet he kept his composure whatever the circumstances and spoke in a low voice, winning the respect of the brothers for his self-control.

Some of the young friars suffered from another malaise which was difficult to treat – homesickness. Maksymilian recounts how the students spent holidays in the small Italian town of Zagarolo at a Franciscan friary set amid orange groves. They went for walks in the countryside and the friars sprawled on the grass looking at the sky and thinking of home. Maksymilian would take from his pocket Sienkiewicz's *Trylogia*, a classic of Polish history which helped them 'to breathe everything that was Polish', and read aloud.

As well as theology and philosophy Maksymilian studied biology, the history of art, mathematics, physics, chemistry and astronomy. His imagination was seized by the sciences and he wrote a monograph to explain the physical and biological possibilities of interplanetary and interstellar travel. His grasp of astronautic science greatly impressed the noted Italian physicist and Jesuit, Gianfranceschi, Professor of Chemistry, Physics and Astronomy at the Gregorian University. He declared that Kolbe could become a pioneer in space. But Maksymilian's talents were already bespoken. He lived an intense life of prayer preparing himself to become a priest. He rarely mentioned himself in his letters to his mother but signs of spiritual growth were plain. On 6 April 1914 he sent her Easter greetings, 'I wish you neither health nor prosperity. Why? Because I want to wish you better than that, something so good that God would not wish you better: that in all things, let his will be accomplished in you, that you may know in all things how to fulfil the will of this very good Father.'

When war came his Polish brothers, who were all Austrian

35

subjects, had to leave, but as a Russian subject he was allowed to stay. He was often sick but always he made light of his illness and rarely asked indulgence because of it. Europe was now enmeshed in the desperate struggles of the Great War; everything fell into a new perspective; there were no signs of peace among the people and one man's health was of small consequence, especially to a member of the Order of Friars Minor.

On All Saints' Day, 1 November 1914, Maksymilian made his solemn profession as a Franciscan. After the gospel reading in the Mass, he made his Perpetual Vows: 'I, Friar Maksymilian Maria Kolbe vow and promise to Almighty God, to Blessed Mary Ever Virgin, to our Holy Father Francis and all the Saints, and to you, Father, to observe for the whole of my life the Rule of the Friars Minor, confirmed by Pope Honorius according to the Constitutions of our Order by living in obedience without property and in chastity.' In reply the Provincial said, 'And I in the name of Almighty God promise that if you observe these things you will have everlasting life.' So at the age of twenty Maksymilian became an apostle of the improbable religion of love brought to the world by Christ and adopted in sublime simplicity by St Francis.

Francis wrote in his Testament, 'Nobody told me what I ought to do; but the Almighty himself revealed to me that I should live according to the formula of the Holy Gospel.' The living Rule of the first Franciscans was Francis himself. They were wandering preachers, without hearth or home, and dressed in rags. They earned their bread by work or by begging when this was insufficient. Of all earthly joys they preserved only that of friendship.

Later Kolbe was to write, 'The principal characteristic of the Franciscan Rule is holy poverty . . . for the Rule's strongbox is bottomless, namely the inexhaustible power of divine providence.'

In 1915 at the age of twenty-one he gained his doctorate in philosophy.

Two years later Maksymilian was diagnosed as tubercular

when he was striken by sickness in the summer of 1917. But making light of the haemorrhages and headaches he started a project which was to become his life's legacy.

In 1917 while celebrating the two-hundredth anniversary of the movement, Freemasons made Rome the forum for vicious demonstrations against the Roman Catholic Church. They brandished banners under the windows of the Vatican showing the devil stamping under foot the archangel Michael. They flaunted flags in St Peter's Piazza which declaimed, 'Satan must reign in the Vatican', 'The Pope will be Satan's slave', and they distributed tracts vilifying the Holy Father.

Maksymilian was moved to take action. His first impulse was to seek permission from his Rector to let him go at once to Palazzo Verde, headquarters of the Freemasons, and convert the Grand Master. The Rector suggested he was perhaps over-ambitious and it would be more realistic to start by praying for the conversion of the Freemasons. Friar Maksymilian did so immediately – he was not a man to vacillate – and next debated with his confrères how to change things. He rallied them, 'In the face of such strong attacks by the enemies of the Church of God, is it enough to complain and weep? No, each of us has a holy obligation to build a trench and personally hurl back the assaults of the foe.' The idea of counter-attack filled his mind.

During morning meditation on 20 January 1917, Father Stephen Ignudi, the Rector of the Seraphic College, dwelt upon the conversion of Alphonse Ratisbonne, a French Jew. A brilliant lawyer and banker, he had found it difficult to forgive the secret conversion of his brother, Theodore, to Christianity. Yet on 20 January in 1842 Alphonse claimed a vision of Mary in the church of Sant' Andrea delle Fratte in Rome which moved him to become baptized himself eleven days later.

In his cell Maksymilian always kept the picture of some saint to whom Mary had appeared, for his ideals had always been dramatically shaped by revelations of the Virgin. Now he listened intently to the story of Ratisbonne's vision and conceived a plan. He would launch an international Militia. Its crusaders would combat the omnipresent evils of the day and consecrate their lives to Mary. The objective would be nothing less than global conquest, his knights would cross all frontiers. He was explicit, 'We have three fronts to conquer. We must first conquer ourselves – this is the most vital front because without this we cannot dream of winning the other two. The second front is our immediate neighbour. The third is the whole of humanity.'

Maksymilian's confrères listened to his large ideas and six had imagination enough to join his crusade as founder members and fellow knights. He counselled them that they should not strive to make a grand formal organization of the Militia but rather an informal movement which would help men and women draw close to God of their own desiring. The knights' task would be to make it easier for men to see God; but the decision to look must be their own.

His good Rector, Father Ignudi, gave his consent for their inaugural meeting. The seven young men, Italians, Poles and Romanians, met behind the closed doors of a cell to decide the aims of a movement which was to spread across the world. They were Father Joseph Pal, priest of the Romanian province; Father Antoni Głowiński, priest of the Romanian province; Friar Jerome Biasi of the Paduan province; Father Quirico Pagnalberi of the Roman province; Friar Anthony Mansi and Friar Henry Granata, both of the Neopolitan province, and Friar Maksymilian himself of the province of Poland. That meeting was on the evening of 16 October 1917, but in the same way as it was customary for evening vespers to belong to the next day's devotions, the anniversary is often recorded as 17 October, the Feast of St Margaret Mary Alacoque. Thus began Maksymilian's Militia.

Long before his ordination an abscess on the thumb of his right hand became gangrenous and doctors decided it must be amputated. The Rector, then Father Bondini, visited him. He told the young friar of his own experience as a boy of twelve when a bone in his foot became infected and his leg was to be amputated. His mother bathed it in Lourdes water and it healed. The Rector gave Maksymilian a bottle containing some Lourdes water and the doctors used it in a compress for his thumb. The next morning the surgeon saw an operation was unnecessary.

On a beautiful spring day in Rome, 28 April 1918, Maksymilian was ordained priest by Cardinal Basillo Pompili at the church of Sant' Andrea della Valle. The following day he celebrated his first Mass at the altar of Sant' Andrea delle Fratte where a plaque records: 'In 1842 the Blessed Virgin appeared to the Hebrew Ratisbonne to transform this fierce wolf into a gentle lamb.'

Kolbe and the founding friars agreed that the new crusade should be known internationally as the Militia Immaculatae (M.I.) and should recognize three degrees of membership. Ironically they adopted nomenclature redolent of the élitist Freemasonry movement. They decided that the First Degree would admit individual members; the Second Degree (M.I.2) would cater for special groups, while the Third Degree (M.I.3) would be 'a truly heroic Degree', mainly for religious. Members' names would be entered in an official register.

There were few rules or stipulations and each member was free to perform his religious duty in daily life according to circumstances, opportunities, talents, zeal and prudence. They also resolved that all knights would wear the 'miraculous medal'. This medal was struck after Catherine Labouré, Sister of Charity of St Vincent de Paul, claimed that the design had been given to her by the Virgin Mary in three visions in 1830. Mary, who appeared standing on the world with rays of incandescent light pouring from her hands, told Catherine to have a medal made depicting the scene, and promised great graces to those who wore it.

During the next nine months Maksymilian sought the counsel of such eminent men as Father Alessandro Basile, the Jesuit Rector of the Pontifical Faculty, to whom the Pope and the College students made their confessions, and the Franciscan Bishop of Amelia, Francis Berti, a wise pastoral leader.

His main confidant, however, was Father Ignudi, his distinguished Rector who was an aesthete, well-known preacher and specialist on Dante. Yet for all this abundance of advice the Militia did not make rapid advances in its first year. Many doubts were voiced and many obstacles arose. Two of the founders, Father Antoni Głowiński and Friar Anthony Mansi, contracted Spanish influenza and died, and Maksymilian himself had a relapse in health and was sent to Amelia, seventy-two kilometres north of Rome, to recuperate. Here during a break from studies, he copied out the aims of the Militia and sent them to the Minister General of the Franciscan Order, Dominic Tavani, seeking his blessing. When the Minister General gave his written approval he added a wistful postcript, 'If only there were twelve of you . . .', for Francis of Assisi and his followers numbered twelve when they went to Rome in 1209 to ask permission to start a brotherhood. It was not until 28 March 1919 that Pope Benedict XV gave his oral blessing through Bishop Dominic Jacquet of the Franciscan Order, then Professor of Church History at the College.

Brother Innocenty, who is now the archivist for the Militia, said that it aimed to make available to everyone the happiness that comes from the presence of God, the first source of all happiness. Maksymilian always said of himself, 'I am the happiest man in the world.'

The blasphemous conduct of the Freemasons in Rome appears to have been the catalyst for the Militia but the sweeping objectives of the new movement must have been influenced by proof of hatred on a wider scale. It represented one unknown friar's revulsion against war and hate by enlisting witnesses to the gospel of peace and love – his motto was always 'love without limits'. By 1917 any glamour attached to war was long tarnished and even fiercer phases of the fighting were envisaged. The year in which Maksymilian had begun his crusade was momentous for two events: America's entry into the war and the Russian revolution which overthrew the Tsarist autocracy.

At eleven o'clock on 11 November 1918 the firing ceased. The democracies of the Western Allies had won the war.

The previous day Józef Piłsudski was released from Magdeburg Fortress in East Germany where he had been interned for the past seventeen months. He returned to Poland with the halo of a hero, his reputation as a redoubtable fighter for independence unsullied. He soon became head of state and commander-in-chief of the Polish Army.

At the Paris Peace Conference in January 1919 the new map of Europe was drawn according to the principles of self-determination and only three per cent of the continent were to live under foreign rule. The Poles were euphoric and exuberant and extravagant in their demands. After a century and a quarter of subjection they had emerged their own masters. No one had dreamed at the outset of war that all the partitioning powers would be defeated. But for four years of butchery and bloodshed Poland had been the main battle arena of the eastern campaigns and the Poles forced to fight variously in the Russian, Austrian and Prussian armies – countryman fired on countryman, the final enormity.

The Peace Treaty was signed on 28 June 1919 and the thirteenth of Wilson's famous fourteen points created an independent Polish State with access to the sea. The dream of independence was realized at last but the awakening was traumatic. A third of the new state comprised national minorities who became increasingly antagonized and confused by the change of policies as Polish governments rose and fell with bewildering speed. The 1921 Polish Census returned 3.9 million Ukrainians, 1.04 million White Russians, 2.85 million Jews and 1.06 million Germans. The numbers of Ukrainians and White Russians were probably understated because of administrative pressure on people to declare themselves as Poles. There was a multiplicity of political parties; some nineteen at Independence in 1918 and an incredible ninety-two eight years later. They produced fourteen different governments during this period.

War damage was heavy, and Polish industry had been

decimated through requisition by the occupying forces. But most people earned their living from the land although farming was largely under-capitalized and inefficient. The country was in economic chaos. There were six currencies circulating and it was not until 1920 that a single currency was established.

In March 1920 Piłsudski proposed an improbable settlement with Soviet Russia which would have recognized Polish dominance in the Ukraine. When this was rejected he formed an offensive alliance with the Ukrainians and on 7 May the two armies seized Kiev, the city of a thousand golden domes. Soviet Russia wanted peace but not at the price of a Polish government in the Ukrainian capital.

In a Soviet counter-offensive the imprudent Poles and their allies were driven back deep into Poland. To the south the Russians advanced two hundred miles to reach Lwów by the end of July while to the north they moved three hundred miles to the outskirts of Warsaw. The Poles launched a counter-attack on the south flank of the Russian force in front of Brest-Litovsk and on 15 August Piłsudski led the Fourth Army in The Battle of Warsaw which penetrated the Russian lines after three days. This encounter is more poetically known as The Miracle of the Vistula, either because the Feast of the Assumption of the Virgin Mary is celebrated on this day, or because it was held that the victory could only have been achieved through divine providence. On 25 August 1920 the Bolsheviks sued for peace, a treaty was finally signed in Riga on 18 March 1921, and a year later Vilna was incorporated into Poland. It was only then that the boundaries were established which were to last until the coming of the Second World War.

In July 1919 Father Maksymilian was recalled to Poland to become Professor of Church History in the Cracow Siminary of Friars Minor Conventual where he had studied seven years earlier. He did not feel strong enough to make the journey and uncharacteristically asked the Father Rector if he might stay in Italy for a little while longer. The Rector was not sympathetic. 'Never mind,' he said, 'you will manage.' Maksymilian reached Bologna and waited for a train to Poland. He was lucky and given a sleeping berth on a comfortable Red Cross train full of returning prisoners-of-war and wounded. It took five days to reach Cracow. He looked out of the windows at the countryside in the short July nights and thought about his future in Poland. His father was dead and he grieved that it was impossible to find his grave. It was five in the morning when he knocked at the door of the Felician Sisters in ul Smoleńsk and asked for his mother. Marianna had not been expecting him. She came full of joy, greeting him by her own fond endearment, Mundzio! He had become Father Maksymilian; she was thankful that she lived to see him a priest and was proud of him. He said Mass in the convent chapel. Marianna knelt in one of the pews and thought with motherly concern how he had changed. He looked undernourished. He was no longer a boy.

It was his mother who became the first member to enlist in the Militia Immaculatae in Poland.

CHAPTER FOUR

Maksymilian must have known both elation and despondency upon his homecoming. Poland was gloriously free of foreign rulers but the country faced daunting problems. Its politics were confused, social conditions chaotic, the economy shattered and inflation soaring. In December 1918 the exchange rate for the Polish mark was 9.8 to the dollar; by the end of 1920 it fetched 579.3, and three years later was to reach an astronomical 2,300,000 marks.

Maksymilian had come a long way since his student days in Cracow. He returned with doctorates in both theology and philosophy and as the originator of an international crusade. He had also made a high resolve. 'I must be a saint – *a great one*', he wrote in a personal memorandum.

A fellow Franciscan, Father Anselm Kubit, records that Kolbe arrived in Cracow 'weak and sickly', but there was a severe shortage of teachers and religious because of the war and an epidemic of influenza, so he began his professorial duties without demur. As well as teaching church history and philosophy he worked unceasingly to build the membership of the Militia. This was the enterprise closest to his heart. The Provincial, Father Ludwik Karwacki, gave his blessing to the undertaking as did Bishop Sapieha of Cracow to whom Maksymilian explained its programme. Without wasting time he established a conclave of knights drawn from the theology students of the seminary, and also organized groups for the friar priests and the lay people. The first of the 'focus groups', as they were known, was for university students, young women studying at religious institutes, and soldiers stationed in Cracow. It was the intellectuals and students who came

44

forward in the beginning but soon large numbers of ordinary people joined, encouraged by Maksymilian's insistence that the Militia was flexible enough to penetrate every sphere of society and that 'the field of work for every knight is his own environment'. Records of those early days showed the wide embrace of a movement which was to outnumber the Franciscan Order itself from which it sprang. Maksymilian marshalled his troops and prepared his tactics with skill, showing much of the enthusiasm and organizational ability of his father Juliusz.

He saw a need to keep in personal touch with the knights who came from such a wide cross-section and dreamed of publishing a monthly bulletin. He would call it *Rycerz Niepokalanej* (The Knight of the Immaculate) and it would keep the knights in touch with him and with each other. The Press, he decided boldly, must be a 'big gun' in his armoury. Before he could further his improbable plan Maksymilian suffered a breakdown and ran a high fever; he was physically and mentally exhausted.

His Superiors sent him to the sanatorium at Zakopane, a health resort and skiing centre in the Tatra Mountains along the southern frontier of Poland. Here in these tranquil surroundings, around the same time as The Miracle of the Vistula was won near Warsaw, Maksymilian recovered after doctors had given him three months to live. Treatment for tuberculosis, or galloping consumption as it was often called, consisted in those times of rest, fresh air and good food. Maksymilian wrote to tell his mother that all day was spent in 'treatment – lying in bed on the balconies and eating as much as possible'.

The hospital was managed by a university 'mutual aid' association and of the many students among the patients only one girl was a practising Catholic. Soon Maksymilian was well enough to mix with fellow-sufferers. He spent much of his time listening and talking to the young people. They had plenty of fresh mountain air but he opened new windows and introduced fresh thoughts. His breadth of interest was a welcome diversion into the tedious routine of the sanatorium, and the students asked him to plan a series of talks. Kolbe goodnaturedly saw his job as not only attacking atheism – or 'freethinking', which was the fashionable term – but combating the annihilating boredom of hospital life. He was well equipped for intellectual sparring with the most brilliant of the students because he was well-read in the sciences as well as philosophy and theology. Father Kolbe was in the van of scientific and technical progress and also in religious thinking, a sphere in which the Polish intelligentsia were often ignorant. His happy nature won friends as well as converts. He became more and more in demand, and gained a rare understanding of the sick which he was never to lose. He would gently entreat doctors and nurses, 'Try to put yourselves in their place.'

Maksymilian welcomed 'his Sister Suffering' in the true Franciscan spirit. In one of his lectures at Cracow he called suffering 'The fire that purifies everything', and later, when a missionary in Japan, he wrote to the brotherhood in Poland, 'All these trials are useful, necessary, and even indispensable, like the crucible where gold is purified.' He made no distinction between men – ordained priests and lay brothers, believers and unbelievers, scholars or artisans – except the sick. Henceforward he treated 'his beloved sick' with unbounded tenderness, summoning the best advice, bearing treats, providing little extras. He solaced them by declaring they were his 'best workers' because they gave so much in prayer. In this way he helped them to overcome a sense of uselessness and of burdening others by their dependence. So he would visit the sick every day of his life.

During his long convalescence the pursuit of holiness was uppermost in his mind, and he wrote to his younger brother, Józef, now a seminarian of his Order who had taken the religious name Alphonsus, on 4 October 1920: 'If you fulfil that which you plan, you will be a saint in a short time. But that is the path to the infinite . . . The faster we run, the more we recognize how slow our pace has been. So it is a matter of beginning anew all the time; as St Francis said on his death-bed: "Let us begin to do good".'

In November 1921 Maksymilian returned to Cracow much improved in health and with his dreams intact. He still cherished hopes of a monthly magazine for which he had already prepared some articles while in the sanatorium. Now he approached the Provincial for permission to publish. It was granted provided that the Province would incur no expense; the Order was poor and could not contribute: he must find the money to finance such a venture himself. His fellow friars must have laughed up the wide sleeves of their habits at such large and impractical ideas which raised so many imponderables.

Maksymilian remained resolute in his plan although he had to steel himself to beg for money. He made a shy and awkward beggar but eventually he had collected enough from the poorest families in the meanest streets to print the first copy. In January 1922 when other well-established newspapers were 'folding' in the Depression, the first edition of *Rycerz Niepokalanej* appeared, financed entirely by the offerings of the poor. The print was 5,000 copies, and now Maksymilian, who was still teaching, had to distribute it. He was a true communicator who wanted to reach the largest possible audience. Whether people could afford to buy the paper was almost immaterial for he would give it away: distribution was his all-important aim. The magazine bore a message on its masthead: 'We cannot guarantee regular editions of this Review due to lack of funds. We are poor but we are not too proud to accept financial help.' The magazine carried sixteen pages and Maksymilian wrote most of it himself.

In the first issue he told readers, 'Everyone cannot become a genius but the path of holiness is open to all . . . It is untrue that the saints were not like us. They too experienced temptations, they fell and rose again; they experienced sorrow that weakened and paralysed them with a sense of discouragement . . . They did not trust themselves but placed all their trust in God.'

He wrote logically and plainly for the ordinary people who were eager to read his simple explanations of the faith, and his short apologetic articles composed in dialogue form were an object lesson in effective communication. It is remarkable how a man of his scholarship could find the right level for his readership who were poor and often ill-educated.

He was determined to sell the magazine cheaply and in large numbers. 'A working person doesn't have time to read trash but a worthwhile and reasonably priced book will find buyers', he declared. His policies were both daring and adroit. He would not take advertisements because he considered space too valuable, but he found it good public relations to send the magazine free of charge to anyone who asked because this prompted many subscribers to pay for those who could not afford copies. He also shamed subscriptions from his readers by gently touching their consciences. He wrote, for example, 'We will willingly offer the magazine free to anyone who is unable to give anything for the work of the Immaculate even by depriving himself a little.'

When he finished distributing the little blue magazine around the streets of Cracow he returned to the friary happy but hardly rich. The problem of financing the magazine became acute. The printing costs for the second issue were also raised by begging, but once the magazine had gone to the printers devaluation of the currency rendered the money almost worthless. The Guardian reproved Maksymilian's improvidence with an old Polish proverb, 'This is what happens, my son, when you try to attack the moon with a spade.'

His mother, Marianna, records these times, 'When he came back from Rome and wanted to edit a monthly paper to the glory of the Immaculate, everyone advised him against it. It would be impossible during the Depression to edit a new paper while other papers were closing down. It was difficult for him to get permission. After printing the first paper he himself distributed it and at the same time he asked tentatively for a little money towards the next issue. But after the second issue he had not enough money to pay the printer's bill. He didn't lose hope. He asked the seminarians to pray with him to the Immaculate because it was her cause.'

Maksymilian decided he would take his troubles to church. He went to the Basilica of St Francis in Cracow where there is an altar dedicated to the Madonna of the Seven Dolours. He sat in the Confessional of the Immaculate and then took Mass. Later before the picture of the Madonna, called 'The Beloved Benefactress', he prayed. Then he noticed an envelope on the altar. It was addressed 'To You, O Mother Immaculate'. He took the letter to the sacristy to open and inside found the exact sum of the printer's bill. The letter read, 'Use this money just as you will. My Immaculate Mother I have nothing worthy of you, but as a proof that I love you frankly I give this little sacrifice. O my beloved Mother, accept it from your child loving you with all the heart.'

In the first year of publication Maksymilian changed printers five times because of rapidly rising costs and frequent strikes. The paper was popular from the first but the difficulties of production were immense. It was plain that Maksymilian needed his own printing press, bigger premises, more labour and much more capital. His Superiors decided that the whole project had outgrown the Cracow friary and in the autumn of 1922 instructed their crusading editor to move the work to the suburbs of Grodno, an ancient oriental city on the Niemen river near the borders of Lithuania.

The friary was large and ramshackle and the Guardian allocated three rooms to the editorial team. The Provincial made Maksymilian a loan, and an American priest, Father Lawrence Cyman, gave a hundred dollars, so soon he had enough money to buy an ancient printing press from a sister order, 'The Nuns of Providence', at Langiewniki near Cracow. The vintage machine, which the friars soon christened 'Old Grandmother', had to be operated manually. It took all a man's strength to turn the handle, and 60,000 revolutions of the wheel to print the 5,000 copies of the magazine. While one man heaved at the handle, another worked the treadle which was an easier task, so the two men would exchange places at frequent intervals. Initially four friars worked on the printing enterprise, including Brother Albert Olzakowski who was a printer. Although his skill was invaluable to the paper, the Provincial had first call on Brother Albert's time, and because of his knowledge of Russian he was often in demand as a secretary. This was important for many official documents were in Russian. The friars spared their editor as much as they could the heaviest exertion because they feared exhausting work would precipitate another haemorrhage. It must have been difficult to stop him because Maksymilian's policy was to ignore his illness and to allow himself no concessions. For all their solicitude he soon had workman's hands and toiled as hard as any of them.

Maksymilian also wished to eliminate class distinction between priests and 'lay' brothers who were still too often seen as inferior and given the most menial jobs. (All members of the Order are referred to as *friars*; it is customary to call the priests *fathers* and those engaged in other works are called *brothers*; all take the same vows and wear the same habit.) Such vestigial patronage lingered from feudal days when there was a strict separation between them. Segregation had officially been abolished around the turn of the century but old attitudes were hard to change. Maksymilian was offended by such religious apartheid. It was a touch of imagination to publish pictures of the brothers in patched religious habit putting the review 'to bed', – preparing it for printing – because the working man was able to recognize himself in these simple worker brothers raised to equal footing with the clerical members of the community. This showed that religious life could be down-to-earth and brought forward many candidates, but they presented a problem by making their own condition: they wanted to work on the paper. The Superiors were nonplussed but deemed it churlish to refuse candidates with such enthusiasm, and were reassured when they saw that Maksymilian was not to be wooed by the technical qualifications of some of the recruits – their devotion to the Immaculate must be paramount. Some of the

50

more conservative members of the Order, though, disapproved of such 'sudden vocations' and suggested that ordinary workmen be employed who would live at home. Maksymilian insisted that only consecrated brothers were suitable; his publishing was no ordinary business venture: 'It is infinitely more than that.' Some of the older friars even criticized the very idea – 'St Francis intended us to preach and hear confessions, not publish papers' – conveniently forgetting that there were no printing presses in his day. At Grodno now the ratio between priests and brothers changed and the new climate created by the Militia helped to make the brotherhood more democratic.

The printing had expanded from three rooms to occupy an entire wing of the friary, which by this time had electric power. Maksymilian bought bigger printing machines which were worked by motor, a linotype machine for setting type, a saw machine and a diesel engine. The magazine paid for much of it but Maksymilian had a flair for getting many of the tools he wanted at bargain prices. The circulation of the magazine increased rapidly, so much so that demand was constantly ahead of supply. Readers asked for back issues and borrowed numbers to copy out. In three of the worst years of the Depression circulation rose from 5,000 to 45,000 copies.

If Maksymilian wanted anything for the printing office he had to ask the Guardian who knew nothing about the work or what it involved. The other constant difficulty was finance. The magazine was now solvent but the money it made was needed to buy new equipment and pay for the friars' upkeep.

Brother Gabriel recalls working on the *Rycerz Niepokalanej* from early days. 'It was a labour of love. We sweated much and often felt our backs were breaking. This complete sacrifice for the Holy Mother was a novelty and it wasn't easy to accept it wholly, so some friars left. It was laborious work but satisfying and there was the pleasure of working with Father Kolbe. He was filled with an extraordinary enthusiasm and everyone saw him as a saint. He was always cheerful; often he laughed until the tears came to his eyes, and he wanted his brothers to be happy because that is the special quality of the Franciscan Order.' Maksymilian did not believe the brethren should be 'sad and sombre like hypocrites' but rather 'joyful and pleasant' as written in the Rule of 1221. Another brother observed, 'While Father Kolbe had the ideas and led us, he never put himself above others and always worked with us.'

The friars at first marvelled that their editor could work so hard, because of his tuberculosis. His posture was affected by his illness so that his arms appeared bent, his back stooped and his head was inclined to one side. His pace was slow and his voice soft. He was of middling height and slim build although his habit made him appear more bulky. His eyes were brown and thoughtful and he had dark hair, later to become grey as did his long beard.

His confrères became accustomed to his bouts of ill-health and, following his example, tried to take little notice. Maksymilian often went to Warsaw on business concerning the paper and to attend to many needs. For example, the large knife for cutting the newsprint had to be sharpened and it could be done only in Warsaw. Sometimes when it was obvious that he was ill, the friars would remonstrate and plead to go in his place, but he would say lightly, 'Don't worry about it. I'll slip in somewhere on the way and get better!' It was as if he were consumed with the feeling that he might not be able to finish the work he had started.

In 1926 his ill-health could no longer be ignored and he suffered such a relapse that he was sent back to Zakopane. The Provincial brought Father Alphonsus to Grodno as acting editor and such was his affinity with his brother that Maksymilian was able to delegate the work and concentrate upon getting well. He had previously printed many of Alphonsus' articles and poems which he found moving and full of meaning. Now Alphonsus became chief editor of the magazine and sales continued to increase. Fellow Franciscans remember Alphonsus as 'brave, energetic, dedicated and full of humility'. There was not much physical likeness between the brothers but they shared the same aims.

When Maksymilian returned after seven months' sickness, he was overjoyed at the way the paper prospered, but he had no intention of resting content. Now that the printing enterprise had proved successful, there was a cleavage of opinion between the journalists and the elderly friars. Maksymilian wished to spend the profits on expanding in the most modern and effective ways, but the friars wanted to put the money in the bank. Such an idea was anathema to Maksymilian who wrote, 'Our greatness is not to be found in amassing material things but rather to be freed from them. The world says: "Blessed are the rich", but Jesus says "Blessed are the poor".'

It had become abundantly clear that such a printing project could not exist alongside an ordinary Franciscan friary. Maksymilian had already decided by 1927 that his publishing house had once again outgrown its accommodation and these conflicts only accelerated the need to move. The circulation of the paper had risen to 50,000 and it had doubled its pages to thirty-two, while the Militia numbered 126,000 knights, including the Minister Provincial, converted from his early scepticism.

CHAPTER FIVE

Maksymilian rejoiced that Church-Government relations had begun to improve. The government set about implementing a Concordat signed with Rome in 1925: it now recognized the dominance of the Church in religious education; government officials began to take part in religious ceremonies, and concessions were made concerning church property. Such improvements followed Piłsudski's coup in the spring of 1926 which was prompted by the continuing chaos on the parliamentary front.

Self-government was a novelty to the Poles, and a nightmare because Poland was too poor for ambitious social experiments. The parliamentary constitution they adopted in March 1921 had been too sophisticated for novices, introducing at once both proportional representation and universal suffrage. Criticisms came from Right, Left and Centre. Piłsudski protested that it had led to an excessive influence of party politics in the army and foreign policy. He resigned as chief of staff when a right wing government came into power in 1923, and went into retirement to bide his time.

The Witos government formed on 10 May 1926 was seen by the Left and by Piłsudski supporters as the start of a right-wing coup against the constitution. They feared it would presage a more authoritarian form of government. On 12 May Piłsudski rode into the suburbs of Warsaw at the head of five regiments. His purpose, in the words of a British historian, was 'to stop the fooling': in his own rather grander words, 'the diminution of robbery and the pursuit of honesty'. After three days of fighting in which about four hundred were killed and nearly a thousand wounded, Piłsudski was victorious.

But he did not wish to establish a dictatorship after the coup. 'Poles cannot be ruled with a whip', he declared. He stood for president to legitimize his power but resigned as soon as elected on the pretext his personality was unsuited to the office – in fact, he regarded it as too limited in authority.

Piłsudski did take the office of prime minister from October 1926 to June 1928 (and was to do so again from August to December 1930), but played little part in day-to-day government. The only office he held continuously after the May 1926 coup was that of minister of war.

A world economic revival began several months after the coup and by seizing power Piłsudski ended the political instability in Poland and boosted business confidence. The government encouraged foreign capital, unemployment fell, and new social reforms extended welfare benefits.

When Maksymilian heard that there was land for sale on the Teresin flats stretching out west of Warsaw, he imagined a huge 'printing village' and heard the purposeful din of presses. The land was in the heart of Poland, near Sochaczew, only forty-two kilometres from the capital city, Warsaw. The marshes and sandy meadows spread opposite the small railway station of Szymanow, and this was crucially important to the Franciscan editors who were beset by distribution difficulties at Grodno. The six-acre plot was the perfect answer to all their prayers, a place of their own where they could publish papers for mass circulation.

The price asked for the land by the owner of the estate, a young Polish noble and large landowner, Prince Jan Drucki-Lubecki, was fair, but the Franciscans were poor: poverty was the holy hallmark of their Order. Maksymilian, though, was a gentle man of granite faith and asked the Prince to offer him the plot. As an earnest of his intent he embedded a plaster statue of the Virgin Mary in the middle of a bare field on 6 August 1927. 'Take possession of this land,' he prayed, 'for I know it is just what you want.'

As a condition for its use by the friars, the Prince required that Masses be offered in perpetuity, but when Maksymilian sought the Provincial's permission he was refused, for his Superior considered such a stipulation would be too onerous. Obediently Maksymilian told Prince Drucki-Lubecki that the transaction was off, but added on impulse that he might keep the statue. The Catholic Prince abruptly changed his mind: he gave the Franciscans the land asking nothing, and the Provincial gave his blessing.

Polish winters come early and frost lay upon the fields in October when the first few friars journeyed from Grodno to make their new home. They came shouldering picks and planks. They carried shovels and hammers and began to build rough huts. The local people were moved by the dedicated toil of the young workmen in their patched religious habits, and before the first hut was built, one of the neighbours, the Jaroszewski family, gave shelter to the small band of brothers. They prepared the one bed they had for Father Kolbe but he chose to sleep on a pallet on wood shavings strewn over the floor and gave the bed to a brother, for he claimed no privileges on account of his priesthood; on the contrary he insisted it behoved him to make the most sacrifices. The good neighbours brought the friars baskets of food and lent helping hands to build a rudimentary friary. Other gifts included wagon-loads of wood, and local farmers transported materials from the station to the site. Sharing bread and work led to such a spirit of community between the 'little brothers' and the peasants that the place came to be called affectionately *our* 'Niepokalanów' (City of the Immaculate).

Maksymilian had recently returned from the tuberculosis sanatorium where doctors had prescribed plenty of food and sleep, no lifting or carrying, a well-ordered life: now he worked as hard as any of his workmen on scant sleep and sparse food. He had rough hands, dusty feet, a torn habit. For the brothers from Grodno, he was another St Francis: it seemed like a second Assisi, where the first companions of Francis sheltered in caves or in huts made of clay and branches of trees, wearing their strange mean clothes.

The earliest constructions were made simply of planks of wood but the main building material was *lesz*, a mixture of slag, cement and lime. It was cheap and easily prepared although pounding it in readiness for use was hard work. Roofs were made of tar paper and there were earth floors. Planks laid across packing cases were used for tables and boxes served as chairs. The brothers drank from tin mugs, ate off tin plates, and slept in crude huts with gaping holes for windows. The wind searched every corner with cutting scorn. In the morning the friars often had to break the ice before they could wash.

On 21 November 1927 the advance party was joined by the rest of the paper's staff from Grodno to erect more substantial sheds for the printing machinery which was on its way by goods train. The printing shop needed brick buildings far superior to the friars' lodgings. Speed of building was important because the move must not interrupt the publication of the monthly magazine. There was another reason for the brothers to work fast. Maksymilian wanted the friary to be consecrated on 7 December for this was the Vigil of the Feast of the Immaculate Conception. He had also decided to make it an 'Open Day' and the brothers had to install the machinery and prepare everything for the public eye. In the words of a Polish saying, the work 'burned their hands': it totally absorbed their energies.

People came to the friary through fields overlaid with peace, their footsteps squeaking in the snow, and looked with wonder upon the poor huts and the plain chapel. Some had criticized the seeming grandeur of Niepokalanów but Maksymilian had replied swiftly, 'Come inside. See just how simply we live.' In the printing shop shining machines stood smartly at attention waiting for orders. The brothers addressed their printing machines as Sister Press, Brother Motor, in the same endearing way as St Francis spoke to the birds and the flowers. Brother

Salezy, who was responsible for the machinery, started the presses; he was anxious about their performance because he had had no time for a trial run but Brother Motor had learned Franciscan obedience; everything ran smoothly. The guests marvelled because it seemed impossible to have created all they saw in so little time. Before leaving they ate simply at the long pine table in the refectory sitting on benches still rough and unplaned.

On the same day the friary was blessed by the Provincial, Father Kornel Czupryk, and Maksymilian addressed the first group of eighteen brother workmen, still without vows, and his own brother, Father Alphonsus. He told them, 'Niepokalanów is the dwelling-place of the Immaculate Mother, chosen by her and consecrated to her honour. Everything here, now and in the future, belongs to her.' Niepokalanów had become the headquarters of Maksymilian's beloved Militia, founded ten years earlier in Rome, whose ranks were increasing steadily. The purposes of the new 'City' were nothing less than to spread the work of the Militia and to convert the world. Its inhabitants, who saluted each other with the greeting, 'Maria!' stood guard over these ideals.

Before leaving Grodno Maksymilian had talked to the brothers about their future in the 'City'. 'In the new friary our consecration must be total. We will observe our Rule, our holy constitutions, and all our prescriptions with complete strictness, for Niepokalanów must be the model of religious life.' He warned them that life would be harsh but the brothers were not apprehensive because they had already become inured to hardship.

Simplicity was to be the touchstone and neither money nor time would be squandered in putting up fine buildings which might invite envy and even requisition by the opponents of religion. In his accounting money lavished on fine buildings would not bring as good a return as money spent developing a fast and efficient Christian press. He kept his vow of poverty absolutely; he and the brothers lived frugally but for God nothing was too costly.

It was no soft life of convenience that he preached; he was a true follower of St Francis who gave his sons the way of apostleship: first came example, preaching was secondary. Maksymilian now set the pattern and encouraged the brothers to persevere in the highest degree of selflessness and a disciplined religious life. The Provincial at first remonstrated that he was making their lives too hard. Maksymilian answered austerely, 'Here there is no room for those in search of comfort and freedom.'

Everything in the 'City' followed the rule of love and there are many testimonies to the affection and solicitude he showed the brothers. One of them wrote, 'I do not think that parents have ever loved their children so much, so providently and so tenderly.' Another said simply, 'I have loved him as much as my own father and mother and even more, for I have found in him both father and mother.' Maksymilian would call the brothers, 'children', 'my children', and everything he had he would share, a warm sweater, overcoat, boots; and although scrupulous in the standards he set and indefatigable in encouragement, he was indulgent and quick to forgive human weakness. Niepokalanów was growing into one large family girded by this bond of love. Maksymilian was sensitively aware that the young men who had joined him to help create Niepokalanów had made real sacrifices, forsaking family, friends and firesides. He said, 'They must find in us a new family.'

Anyone could take his problems to Father Kolbe whose small office was in the heart of the 'City'. It was furnished sparsely with functional objects: clock, scissors, blotter, paper-knife, pigeon-holed shelving for his files, and, of course, a globe and statue of the Virgin Mary. One brother records, 'He had an immense gift for organization and the funny thing was that although there was such a lot of work done, whenever one walked into his office his desk was cleared of papers.' But some of those around him worried that they could not cope with the pace he set and Maksymilian would chide them gently, 'Nothing in the world is worth getting agitated about

59

because you cannot do any proper work if you are anxious.' He would add with marvellous hope, 'Just a little prayer to the Virgin Mary will very likely do the trick – if only by calming you down – she won't do the work for you!'

Despite the non-stop activity prayer always preceded action and spiritual exercises were not neglected. Fr John Burdyszek, who studied for six years at Niepokalanów, and was later to found the English Crusade, said 'Father Kolbe's "five minutes" for Our Lady became well-known in the "City". We do not meditate for one hour, only a little time, about five minutes. But the five minutes must be during a time of peak activity and greatest distraction, so that the greatest effort of will and concentration is needed.' Father Kolbe was fond of repeating, 'This life is short, we must behave like misers, and take the fullest advantage of the time left to us.'

Maksymilian often reflected on the character and quality of prayer. 'Prayer is not better when it gives consolation,' he said, 'but rather when it exacts greater fidelity to return to what you're doing.' He saw prayer as the raising of the soul to God; it was not constantly whispering words. 'The spirit of prayer will fill the soul that is lifted to God, and in practice is the uniting of our will with God's.' His prayer began with 'Thy Kingdom come' and he would insist that a prayer must not be a petition of personal wants. 'Do not ask anything for yourselves, only for others', he told the brothers. 'But if you do happen to pray for yourselves ask only for perseverance in the work for Mary Immaculate.' He would add disarmingly in a matter-of-fact voice, 'I expect you to be saints and very great saints, because sanctity is not a luxury but a mere duty according to Christ's teachings.'

In the little free time they all had they played chess and Maksymilian was apt to win every game. He was delighted.

In the next three years Niepokalanów expanded rapidly, combining medieval austerity with twentieth-century technology. The atmosphere was purposeful and prayerful, cheerful and charitable. Every year the Prince gave permission for them to move the fences to extend their boundaries. In great measure Niepokalanów became self-sufficient.

The community made all the clothes they needed: there were workshops for brother tailors, shoemakers, hatters, stocking-makers. They did not have their own farm because it would have diverted too much labour from publishing: but their dependence on local farmers helped to cement a communal spirit and shared purpose. Every autumn some of the brothers would set forth with carts to collect food like the begging friars of early centuries. They would return from the outlying farming districts with grain, potatoes, carrots, cabbages and beets. Excellent jams and preserves were made from beets and the neighbouring forests supplied hundreds of pounds of raspberries and blueberries for the friary's stores. They had their own infirmary and the sick were surrounded with solicitude. Those seriously ill were sent to the best hospitals in the country and only lesser illnesses treated at Niepokalanów. Some minor operations were performed by brother physicians under the supervision of a surgeon from Warsaw, and teeth were treated by brother dentists.

The brothers were sometimes hungry despite the generosity of farmers, and bills for newsprint, printing ink and postage hung like dark clouds over the 'City'. Maksymilian, however, was never cautious on account of material difficulties, and always unexpected gifts settled the debts. He was devoted to the work of the Militia and he would never wait to buy machinery or building materials he could not afford. It took a particular kind of courage for a Franciscan priest to run into debt but he was optimistic that the means would be forthcoming.

Marianna Kolbe, in her rounds of the tradespeople of Cracow while shopping for the everyday needs of the convent, never failed to ask for 'a little contribution for my son's work at Niepokalanów'. She was tireless and persuasive on his behalf and the pockets of her big black coat would bulge with the money she collected. He wrote to her often but his letters

61

were brief: he asked her to understand that his work was the reason for such brevity and to accept this shortcoming as 'a little sacrifice for the Immaculate'.

Maksymilian had his critics: many objected to the expense of his machines. But he would argue that all inventions must be exploited for the greatest glory of God; the devil should not be allowed all the best tunes. He was fascinated by anything resembling a machine and craved speed in production and transport. Yet he always relegated machinery to its rightful place: machines must serve men and not be their masters.

The workmen were exceptional technicians: according to Warsaw professionals four of the thirty brother linotypists had the highest rating in Poland for setting the type, and those who showed outstanding talent were sent for further training in Warsaw, Poznań and abroad. Polish industry even adopted a number of inventions from Niepokalanów. One of the brothers patented an electric automatic addressograph which won first prize at the Poznań Trade Fair. There was a box in the 'City' inviting suggestions for increasing production and improving quality, and this sharing of ideas enhanced the spirit of oneness which united them. A true democracy was practised because Niepokalanów was their common creation.

The publishing house was to become one of the most modern printing works in Poland for the presses were of the most up-to-date design and of the best manufacture, mostly from Germany. Yet Maksymilian saw no offence against Franciscan poverty. When Cardinal Aleksander Kakowski, Archbishop of Warsaw, visited Niepokalanów he wondered with bemusement what St Francis would say if he saw such splendid and expensive machinery in use by friars. Maksymilian answered without hesitation, 'If St Francis lived he would surely roll up his sleeves and join us.'

In the early days of Niepokalanów, the many wooden buildings made fire a real hazard so the friars organized their own Voluntary Fire Brigade – probably unique in the world

– which later, at the height of anti-religious feeling in Poland was seen as a security measure against sabotage. From the start it ran efficiently. Brother Cherubin, one of the first brother firemen, remembers those pioneering days. A soldierly cheerful man with the rosy cheeks of a boy, and large capable hands, he told how Father Kolbe took a personal interest in the work of the Brigade. The machines and apparatus fascinated him and every time they returned from a summons, he would ask eagerly for technical details of how the fire was controlled. Brother Cherubin recalls how this was the one exception for reversing Kolbe's rule of prayer before action. 'We would put out the fire first and then the order went forth, *Pray*', he said. The firemen would cross themselves and offer a prayer of thanksgiving. The Brigade was appreciated throughout the neighbourhood, and it was remarkable that there was never an accident caused by the friars clambering up and down ladders in their loose and bulky habits. 'We would tuck them into our boots and the only uniform we put on was a fireman's belt and helmet.' It is on record that several times before the Second World War agents infiltrated Niepokalanów and twice set fire to the buildings.

In 1929 a minor seminary was opened at Niepokalanów for boys wishing to become future priests in the Franciscan Order. Here they were educated at secondary school level in ordinary school subjects as well as religious studies in readiness for a year's novitiate if they decided to persevere. The pupils slept in two dormitories with fifty beds in each. Heating came from army type stoves in the middle of the room and two boys took shifts to keep them fuelled. There were metal bowls for washing, and in the refectory the food came on tin plates which became somewhat mutilated. The Superior once asked the brother cooks if they could not change the dishes; he was finding them monotonous. The next day he was astonished to find the mutilated tin plates replaced by new crocks containing similar food.

When Father Kolbe visited the classroom he would ask typically, 'Have you any difficulties?' It appeared that there was often confusion in the minds of the seminarians about devotion to the Virgin. Father Kolbe would retell the story of the Annunciation when Mary spoke with angels and accepted the will of God with the words, 'Behold the handmaid of the Lord.' In a letter to Niepokalanów when on his travels, Maksymilian once wrote, 'Please tell the dear brothers that they should never be concerned that they might love the Immaculate too much, for we will never love her as much as Jesus. And after all, the imitation of Christ is the source of all our holiness.'

By the end of 1929 Niepokalanów, barely two years old, was deemed a model industrial concern and its workers had won renown for their sanctity. Its progress had been phenomenal. But the founder of it all had amazing ambitions: he felt hemmed in, cocooned in a spiritual claustrophobia: his message was not for one town, one country, but for the world. For him Niepokalanów was only the arsenal.

CHAPTER SIX

When Maksymilian asked permission to embark on a mission to Japan his Superiors must privately have judged the new plan to be preposterous. Yet they were reluctant to forbid him. For no one likes to be cast in the role of God's arbiter, and Maksymilian never argued but always submitted docilely to the decisions of his Superiors as coming direct from the Almighty.

Several months earlier he had met some Japanese students on a train, and by combining a number of languages they had managed to talk. On parting they exchanged gifts: Maksymilian gave them 'miraculous medals' – he always carried a supply of his 'bullets' as he called them – and they gave him wooden carvings of elephants. He could not forget these students and he now considered Niepokalanów sufficiently established to leave in the charge of his own brother, Father Alphonsus. On 26 February 1930 Maksymilian left with four chosen brothers for Japan. They did not know the language, they had little money, they had no Japanese friends. They were poor and humble and yet they went with ambitious dreams and the certainty of realizing them.

The five Polish Franciscans crossed France, embarking at Marseilles for the Far East, and during the seven weeks' voyage Maksymilian began to study the confusion of characters in the Japanese language.

Breaking their journey at Shanghai, they were warmly received by La Pa Hong, one of the richest men in China, whose family had been Christians for some three hundred years. He told them that he already had a printing works which they could use and he would build a friary. But when

Maksymilian, overjoyed by such generosity, went to see the Bishop of Shanghai, he was told that the Catholic Congress of 1926 would not allow a newcomer to start work in the Province. He left two of his companions in the city to study Chinese and try to recruit 'knights' before continuing his journey with the two remaining brothers. On 24 April 1930 they landed in the beautiful southern city of Nagasaki, the San Francisco of Japan.

The traditional ancient religion of Japan is Shintoism, 'the religion of a million gods': the word comes from *shin* (god) and *tō* (way). Shinto combined nature worship and ancestor worship and evolved into reverence for the Emperor and Japan itself. But the old primitive religion later became mixed with the more sophisticated Buddhism, the practical philosophy of Confucius, and then with Christianity following the mission of St Francis Xavier, one of the seven founding fathers of the Jesuits who sailed to Japan in a pirate ship in 1548. The new Christian faith met a great need after several centuries of civil war and was accepted by lords as well as peasants.

The open embrace for Christianity was however, short-lived. One of Japan's most powerful generals, Hideyoshi, began to suspect that this foreign religion was but a cover for foreign aggression and political ambitions and might undermine the loyalty of subordinates. In 1587 Hideyoshi issued a decree banning Christian missionaries from Japan but he did little to enforce it for ten years. In 1597 he became angered by the friction between Portugese Jesuits and Spanish Franciscans and on 5 February that year nine missionaries and seventeen Japanese Christians were executed. Hideyoshi died a year later and Tokugawa Ieyasu became supreme ruler. At first he allowed some missionary activities and then his attitude hardened and he announced a law suppressing both preaching and practice of the Christian faith. He was influenced by increasing numbers of converts among his own henchmen whose loyalty he doubted, and the rivalries be-

66

tween Jesuits and Franciscans. He also believed that the Church had acted as the 'spearhead' of imperial conquest in other parts of the world. Ieyasu died in 1616 and his son and successor, Hidetada, proved even tougher in his dealings with Christians. A test of fidelity was introduced for Christian 'suspects' who were ordered to stamp publicly on the face of Christ. Those who refused died atrocious deaths and the Church was driven underground.

The climax of the persecutions came with the Shimabara rebellion in 1637 when Christian peasants near Nagasaki rebelled against economic and religious oppression and were massacred. Two years later Japan was virtually isolated: no Japanese was allowed to go abroad; foreigners were forbidden to settle in Japan, and overseas trade was impossible. Christianity was believed to have been expunged.

Yet two centuries later when Japan was open to the outside world once more, and foreign missionary activities resumed, Christians came out of hiding. They had been practising the faith that had been handed down to them in secret over generations, family teaching family. Some leading Japanese of the day believed that Western ecclesiastical organization was inappropriate to Japanese culture, and the 'non-church' movement was born. Its Christian influence spread to become disproportionate to the numbers of formal church members. When Maksymilian arrived in Nagasaki in 1930 there were 93,000 Catholics in the Japanese Empire among a population of 84 millions.

Typically Maksymilian wasted no time and within hours of landing at Nagasaki with Brother Zeno and Brother Hilario he was conferring with Bishop Hayasaka who found his intentions whimsical and unrealistic. This Polish priest, who had just arrived, did not know the language; he was largely ignorant of national culture and custom; he had no money; yet he wanted to publish and distribute a Catholic magazine in Japanese. Maksymilian humbly begged permission. Poverty was no problem to the providence he trusted; in fact, poverty was a reliable partner in all his unlikely projects. When the Bishop learned he had two doctorates, he looked at his visitor with fresh interest because he was short of professors in his seminary. Maksymilian seized his chance to barter: he offered to take courses in philosophy and theology if the Bishop would allow the publication of the Review. The bargain was struck, and a month later a telegram reached the astonished community at Niepokalanów announcing the printing of the first edition of *Seibo no Kishi* (Knights of the Immaculate) which appeared at first as an addition to the local diocesan magazine.

The language presented acute difficulties, but these were overcome by patience and goodwill. Maksymilian was fluent in German, Italian, Latin, French and Russian, and he had friends of many nationalities who helped him translate his articles into Japanese from the languages he commanded.

The Polish brothers lived simply in a derelict hut with a leaking roof, cooking meagre meals in the open air. There is something innate in the Japanese character that esteems self-sacrifice; by the brothers' singlemindedness and selflessness they won Japanese respect which at once turned to practical help from those both with and without religious faith. An unofficial 'Friends of the Friars' came into being. Soon there was enough money to buy a printing press and it was installed in a tumbledown building which formerly housed Amemori hospital. There were no beds and they slept on the floor and on one occasion the ceiling fell on them. The tables and chairs were so dilapidated that they were suitable only for firewood.

They had great difficulty in getting the magazine printed because Japanese printers continually raised the prices; so Maksymilian decided that the brothers must print it themselves despite the intricacies of typesetting thousands of strange characters. They produced the November number and made history in Japanese printing for this was the first time that a publication had been set by foreigners. Distribution presented other problems. Maksymilian could not repeat

68

the methods he had adopted in Poland of giving away free copies unsolicited; to send a copy to a Japanese home without the owner giving some nominal consent would be regarded as rude. Maksymilian was quick to perceive the strict rules of social etiquette which ordered Japanese conduct and he was punctilious in observing them. Thus a team of his volunteers toured the city, and would approach a stranger in the street with utmost politeness and offer him a copy of the paper: if the paper was accepted and a visiting card produced, then the canvassing of a subscription could proceed. The brothers also advertised in trains, streets and public places, and interested Japanese would send a postcard with their address.

There were many critics who claimed that the new magazine was badly written, full of mistakes and of a low standard. It was readers, though, who mattered to Maksymilian rather than critics, and the response was encouraging, for more and more people were asking for instruction in the faith. The brothers printed 10,000 copies of the early issues.

Maksymilian reported on the progress of the Japanese mission to the brothers in Poland, and to economize on paper he wrote diagonally across his letters in a different coloured ink.

Less than two months after he reached Japan, Maksymilian was recalled to a meeting of the Polish Provincial Chapter of the Franciscans in Lwów. He was reluctant to leave his young enterprise, so tender a shoot, but he had to obey the summons because the Chapter was to discuss the future of the Japanese mission. The Fathers debated the cost of such a commitment and its apparent foolishness. Maksymilian spoke from the heart about the need for the work, and then, characteristically, put his hands under his capuche. While the talking went on he said his prayers, fingering the rosary which he always carried in the watch-pocket of the habit, and waited calmly for the Chapter's ruling. He returned to Japan with authority to continue the Review and to found a Japanese 'Niepokalanów'. Two more brothers accompanied him.

When he reached Nagasaki he found the magazine had not

been published for a month and that his mission was in danger of disintegrating: his fears had been realized; he had left the new venture at a critical stage in infancy. He set to work at once, not only to regain lost ground, but to make rapid and dramatic advances. He began to search for a place where he could build a friary, chapel and printing centre, and a small minor seminary. He had few material resources apart from his loyal band of brothers.

Six months later Maksymilian suffered the loss of his blood brother, Alphonsus. On the eve of the Feast of the Immaculate Conception, 7 December 1930, he had a cable from Poland to tell him that his brother had died suddenly. He had been taken to a Warsaw hospital suffering from a burst appendix. It was a great loss for Niepokalanów where Alphonsus had succeeded Maksymilian as Guardian. He was also editor of *Rycerz Niepokalanej* and he was in such accord with his brother's ideas that Maksymilian could delegate in confidence that everything would be carried out as he wished. Alphonsus was buried in the cemetery in the capital and it was not until after the war that his body was brought for reburial at Niepokalanów. He was succeeded in the 'City' by Father Florian Koziura, rector of the minor seminary.

After some months of searching Maksymilian found a place to build the Japanese 'Mugenzai no Sono' (Garden of the Immaculate) on the outlying hills of Hikosan, The Echo of the Mountain, at Hongochi. For several centuries this land had been used as a cemetery for untouchables. It was believed that ghosts inhabited the area and nobody would buy it. Father Kolbe liked it, especially for its cliffs where it would be ideal to build a Grotto to Our Lady of Lourdes. Many friends and brothers were disconcerted by the choice of such a mountainous location and tried to persuade him to build a friary more conveniently in the heart of the city where an alternative site was offered him. But Maksymilian was insistent, despite the apparent logic of their argument, that he had found the right place, and for some 7,000 yen he bought the six acres of land in the lee of the mountain which dominates Nagasaki. It was like a jungle and to clear the ground was laborious work; it was covered with Japanese cane and tangled undergrowth. Four new brothers – Maksymilian's 'reinforcements', as he termed them – came from Poland to help.

They put up the first huts and moved to their new home on 16 May 1931. It was a spring day filled with shy sun and hopefulness although the previous day it had rained ceaselessly. Once again the conditions were primitive. 'We sleep on straw as we did at Niepokalanów', the friars wrote home. 'We eat from branches and sit on the ground. The poverty is extreme but we are happy.' Maksymilian continued to teach in the diocesan seminary although it meant a tedious journey from the hillside to the centre of the city. A professor visited the brothers several times a week to give language lessons, for the complexities of Japanese are formidable and the grammar has a long and complicated construction. Both the root and ending of a verb may change depending on your style of speech, the honorific, the humble, the polite or plain, and in writing, other forms again may be required. Nor was the technical difficulty of learning the language the only problem. The Japanese found misuse of their language painful and disrespectful, but never amusing. Maksymilian was determined that the brothers must persevere because for making genuine friends a good knowledge of the language was essential.

The magazine gained in popularity. Already in 1931 it was the most widely distributed Catholic periodical printed in a non-Catholic country, and by the end of the first year it had doubled its circulation, printing 20,000 copies. Maksymilian wanted to hire speed-boats to distribute the paper around the islands but this was impracticable to realize so it was sent by post. Many Japanese wrote letters of appreciation to the editor and Maksymilian read them to the brothers to encourage them in their demanding work. Again, as in Poland in the early days of *Rycerz Niepokalanej*, back numbers were eagerly sought. The paper fulfilled its purpose and taught the tenets of Christian doctrine simply by stories. The strength of the Militia also grew and an increasing number of Japanese joined the community.

Maksymilian had many visitors, intellectuals, labourers, university students, children, Buddhist monks; and one room was used as an oratory where they all sat crosslegged on the floor for long discussions. Some missionaries made the mistake of dogmatism, imposing their opinions too zealously, insensitive to other convictions and another culture. Despite his sense of urgency Maksymilian respected other views and it was his willingness to listen and to discuss which won Japanese friendship. It was their custom to talk until the question resolved itself through general consensus and he was content to allow the time necessary. Japanese committees, for example, rarely put a question to the vote; it was a gradual process of talking until the general feeling was finally determined.

A police officer called Yoshino infiltrated the monastery as a spy the following year (1932). He was implanted by the Japanese authorities because of Poland's border with communist Russia. Yoshino, living the same life as the brothers, was moved to reveal his identity and became baptized. His photograph is kept in the friary.

In spite of his worsening ill-health – frequent migraine attacks, bouts of fever, abscesses and shortness of breath – Maksymilian decided by the spring of 1932 that it was time for new 'invasions'. The work in Japan was going well. The magazine had reached a circulation of 60,000 and was widely distributed throughout Japan, attracting many to the Church. He had time to look at the map of the world above his desk. It was India that beckoned and the Provincial gave his blessing. On 29 May he sailed, stopping at Singapore to discuss preparation for a Malayan Review. In India he was received coolly at the residence of the Catholic Archbishop at Ernakalam. In a corridor of the Archbishopric he knelt before the statue of one of his favourite saints, St Thérèse of Lisieux, to pray that she would patronize his work. A rose petal fluttered at his feet from the vase at the base of the statue. He was not surprised when all the difficulties in India were smoothed out and the Archbishop wrote officially to the Franciscan Order inviting the Polish missionaries to proceed. But Maksymilian was not in the Far East to hurry the arrangements and the Community delayed because of the rumblings of war.

A year later in the spring of 1933, Maksymilian was recalled for a second time to the Provincial Chapter to give an account of the Japanese Mission, and tour Polish cities explaining the aims of the work. He returned to Japan with Father Cornelius Czupryk, ex-Provincial, and a novice in the mission field. They were welcomed at Nagasaki harbour on 4 October, the Feast of St Francis, by a large crowd including many children who called Maksymilian affectionately *Ojiisan*, grandfather. Offers of help continued to pour into 'The Garden' and in the same year work began on a beautiful chapel. The five founding friars had grown to twenty-four in three years, a seminary was opened and in six years there were twenty Japanese studying for the priesthood in the Franciscan Order.

It was Christmas in Niepokalanów and the friars had rehearsed one of the traditional nativity plays, the *Jaselka* for all to watch. After supper Father Kolbe said there would be a special conference with him for any who wished to stay behind in the refectory. The *Jaselka* was popular and only a few brothers remained. Maksymilian spoke quietly restraining emotion. Firstly he told them that he was their father even more truly than their own father, because from him they had received their spiritual life and religious vocation. That was why he spoke to them familiarly as 'my children'. He was much older than they were and would not be with them always, so wished to give them a legacy in the shape of a secret. He spoke of the peace and joy he knew from God which could not be expressed in ordinary words but dwelt with him despite the anxieties of life. After some hesitation

73

he went on to say that he had had an intimation while in Japan that heaven had been promised to him in all certainty. The brothers urged him to tell them more: perhaps he had had a vision of Mary. He refused to reveal more; he had only told them because he thought it might be a strength in the trials ahead. 'I am so happy', he whispered. 'Remember then what I have told you and learn to be ready for the greatest sacrifices. My sons, do not wish for extraordinary things, but simply to perform the will of the Immaculate which is the will of God.' He enjoined silence upon each of them. 'As long as I live speak nothing of it.'

The date of this experience in Japan is not recorded but in one of his letters from Mugenzai no Sono, Maksymilian wrote to Niepokalanów, 'God gives us this white ladder and wills that we use it, to scale the heights to come into his presence. This is only poetic imagery: the reality is incomparably more beautiful.'

The health of Poland's ageing marshal, Piłsudski, began to deteriorate in the years after 1926. On 23 April 1935 an Austrian specialist summoned to attend him diagnosed cancer of the liver and stomach, and on 12 May, the ninth anniversary of the coup, Piłsudski died. His body was buried in the cathedral crypt in Cracow in company with Polish kings, and his heart was buried with the body of his mother in Vilna. Much of the country was grief-stricken and shocked for rumours about the gravity of his illness had been denied. Although Piłsudski played small formal part in the Government during the last few years of his life, his mere presence on the public stage had preserved some political unity. His successors could not assume his authority or exercise his charismatic influence.

It was in May of the same year, 1935, that the Polish Catholic daily, *Mały Dziennik* ('Little Daily'), a national newspaper long dreamed of by the Franciscan editors, was first printed at Niepokalanów. It resembled any other national paper with articles about politics, current affairs, sport, culture and comic strips, as well as carrying religious news and comment. Its giveaway price of five groszy (about ½p) was pivotal because Maksymilian wanted even the poorest to read it. It was edited by Father Marian Wójcik, who was a lecturer in philosophy and had taken a course of journalism in Switzerland. The paper was blue and white, the colours of the Madonna, and had an initial run of 17,000 copies daily, reaching nearly 100,000 by the end of the year. It was to expand fast to become the largest newspaper in Poland, printing eleven editions.

The observances of prayer and piety were not overlooked. The night shift ended its work at 5.00 a.m. Then with all Niepokalanów its workers took part in meditation, prayers and Mass; they ate supper and went to bed while the day shift took over the presswork. Before resuming work at 9.00 p.m. the night shift again joined in meditation and evening prayers. Every important plan was supported by prayers. Other newspaper proprietors were both critical and envious; their newspapers were going bankrupt and this 'cabbage leaf' as they called it in contempt, was selling more and more copies.

In May 1936 Maksymilian was recalled to Poland for the general meeting of the Provincial Chapter who once more elected him Guardian of the friary he had founded. There were now some five hundred religious and one hundred and forty seminarians, and it was decided by the Order that a man of Maksymilian's stature and organizational grasp was needed at its head. He was sad to leave for he had grown to love Japan and her people. Doctors had told him more than once that he should return to Poland to save his life because his health was too precarious for such arduous missionary work. They pronounced it a medical mystery that a man of such physical frailty could work so hard. Maksymilian paid no attention to the doctors; he had lived for many years with the verdict of death and did not allow it to bother him; besides he knew that a special death was his destiny. But he had to obey his superiors, although before he left he made his fourth vow – he would return at once if wanted.

A month earlier the minor seminary for Japanese vocations was opened and seminarians came from afar, many of them descendants of early Christians. Upon his return Maksymilian found the degree of organization to be extraordinary; the task had been entrusted to several brothers who had been especially trained in a scientific approach to work techniques. All facilities and manpower at Niepokalanów were divided into twelve divisions with between three and ten sub-divisions. The assignment to the different divisions was based on American tests of natural abilities and each division had its own 'school' so that the brothers quickly achieved professional standards.

The production section was in the heart of the city and its work consisted of preparing copy for the publications which now served millions of readers. As well as the national daily and the monthly review, which reached Poles living abroad as well as at home, there was now *The Little Knight* for youth and another version for young children. *The Calendar of The Knight of the Immaculate* was popular, selling more than a million. Other publications such as *Niepokalanów Echo* and *Enclosure of the Immaculate*, were mostly for members of Niepokalanów. Editorial and circulation branches of Niepokalanów were located in major Polish cities. A separate press agency gathered news items from all over the world and dispatched them in several languages. Books were also published as well as periodicals.

Niepokalanów was now the backbone for the developing Japanese Mission. They prepared 'reinforcing troops' – brothers and priests, supplied medicines and funds; and organized exhibitions and mission days. A separate minor mission seminary prepared young men who wanted to work for the priesthood overseas and the brothers learned foreign languages and trades necessary in mission work.

Another pivotal section was the Direction of Mailing whose job was to get the 'City's' products to its customers as quickly as possible. Such goods included papers, books, pictures, statues, miraculous medals, and used stamps for philatelists. The best routes were planned and despatch organized to the smallest villages and most remote parts of the country, and, indeed, to anywhere in the world.

Other important sections administered the Militia in Poland and abroad; catered for the worldly needs of Niepokalanów; offered library and research facilities; and provided technical workshops. There was a 'security' force and a communications division responsible for an internal railroad system, trucks and cars, road building and repair.

The Order bought a fleet of bicycles to get around the 'city'. Niepokalanów as a friary now spread over seventy-five acres and included a pine tree park planted by the brothers, a vegetable garden, two great ponds to help fire-fighting, and some thirty buildings. There was an electric sawmill, a plant for food processing, a power plant and, as well as the noviate, an athletics stadium. The friars did not spend all their time in prayer and work: time was made for sport which included soccer, basketball, archery and swimming.

An average of two hundred candidates a year were coming to Niepokalanów to seek admission as brothers and those who proved a true vocation were assured by Maksymilian that there was room for everyone. He was well pleased by the atmosphere he had striven to create. It was a workers' republic where everyone from the Guardian to the youngest boy in the minor seminary lived in brotherliness and concord. The neighbours too felt part of the friary they had helped to create, whose lights could now be seen from afar all night long. It had become the custom on Sunday afternoons for six hundred or more brothers in their black habits to walk through the nearby park where the private rosary of the brothers was converted into prayers in the open with joyful participation of the neighbourhood.

In 1937 Maksymilian drew up a five year plan with all the thoroughness of a full-scale military exercise, for the greater order and efficiency of the beloved 'City'. It was intended both to strengthen the spiritual life of the brothers and to expand the work still further. It seemed he had intimations of the sufferings which lay ahead. From Japan came news that in May the country had begun its attempted conquest of China and the Japanese brothers had to join the army. The publications were stopped; the seminary was converted into a detention camp for enemies of the country, and the seminarians were forced to work in munitions factories. The Polish priests and brothers were sent to a detention camp near Mount Aso in Kumamoto Prefecture. In 1938 *Miles Immaculatae* was published, a quarterly in Latin for priests throughout the world. In the same year a short-wave radio station (SP3 RN) Polish Station 3 Radio Niepokalanów, began to broadcast talks and church music. Niepokalanów by 1939 had become one of the largest and most influential religious communities in the world with 762 friars, including 122 young men in the mission seminary. In the spring of that year Maksymilian went to Latvia to prepare for a Niepokalanów, and sent a delegation to Belgium with the same purpose. Petitions asking him to start new 'Cities of the Immaculate' were arriving from all over the world. Father Maksymilian, at the centre of it all, remained poor and modest. He had no wardrobe in his cell but he now planned to build an airport at Niepokalanów, and he sent two brothers to Warsaw to train as pilots. He was also hoping to produce Catholic films with the best actors. All these momentous plans were postponed because of the rumblings of war, for throughout the nineteen thirties the grotesque shadow of the swastika lengthened across Europe.

CHAPTER SEVEN

Shortly before 6.00 a.m. on Friday, 1 September 1939 Germany invaded Poland. Three weeks afterwards at a dinner-party in Hitler's apartment it was resolved between soup and coffee that all representatives of the Polish intelligentsia were to be exterminated. The Führer's guests to discuss these murderous plans were Hans Frank, destined to become Governor General of Poland, and Baldur von Schirach, Head of Reich Youth and later Governor of Vienna.

Frank, who became known as 'the butcher of Poland', was the Nazi Party's leading lawyer and throughout the nineteen thirties drafted most of the Nazi legislation. Now his orders were explicit: 'ruthless expansion of the Third Reich . . . reduction of entire Polish economy to absolute minimum necessary for bare existence . . . the Poles shall be the slaves of the greater German World Empire.' He had stomach enough for the job. His confessed ambition was to make sure that 'the backbone of the Poles is broken for all time', and he admitted he was 'simply not interested in whether the Poles ate or not'. They could have the crumbs from the Germans' table. As a disciple of the Führer Frank rewrote the law and declared 'justice is whatever benefits the German people, injustice whatever harms them'.

So began the crucifixion of Poland, in which crimes against humanity were committed on an escalating scale. They were more savage and calculated than anything in the history of Europe, and yet there are people today who in wishful blindness refuse to believe that such unimaginable crimes were committed. In six years a third of the population of Poland was murdered, and of three million Jews only some three hundred thousand survived. Priests suffered even more than most; between a third and a quarter were killed.

At the Nuremberg Trial in 1945 Hans Frank was convicted from the evidence of the thirty-eight volumes of his diary in which he recorded meticulously and jubilantly carrying out his orders. After his arrest he became a Roman Catholic, and before death by hanging he cried, 'The guilt of Germany cannot be erased in a thousand years'. He spent much time during the trial in prayer and in tears.

The defendants at Nuremberg were called by American prosecutor Mr Justice Jackson, 'twenty broken men'. As individuals their fates were of small consequence to the world, but they were living symbols of racial hatred, terrorism, and the arrogance and cruelty of power. Their crimes were so vile, so malignant, that civilization could not ignore them because it could not survive their repetition. Towards the end of the six-million-word trial, Mr Hore Belisha, former British Secretary of State for War in the Chamberlain Government, compared Nuremberg with the coming to pass of some biblical prophecy.

For a long time Maksymilian had been preparing his peace-loving community for the terrors of war. It was as if he had foreseen the holocaust and its consequences. In 1938 at a meeting of newspaper editors in Poland, he had told fellow-journalists that he was certain there would be war and that he would not survive. He also predicted accurately the post-war boundaries of the country; all western parts would return to Poland including Gdańsk, Szczecin, and Wrocław. He was to repeat this prophecy once to the brothers. A week before the invasion of the country he spoke to the friars in a homily at Niepokalanów about the three stages of life: preparation, activity, and suffering. 'I think the third stage will be my lot shortly. I'd like to die in a knightly manner . . . I wish the same for you. For what nobler can I wish you? Christ himself said, "Greater love hath no man than this, that he lay down his life for his friends."'

When war came Maksymilian sent many of the brothers

80

home to their families. Other brothers, acting upon his advice, volunteered for the Polish Red Cross (PCK). As their Guardian and father he blessed each in tender farewell. He told them, 'The war front is approaching us and the inhabitants of the Sochaczew district must evacuate, including Niepokalanów. Many of you will not return here, and I, most likely, will not live through this war.' By way of consolation he urged them all to remember, 'Niepokalanów is not buildings nor machines, but souls committed to the cause of Christ.'

Out of more than seven hundred friars, only thirty-six remained at the friary, which opened its gates to refugees and the sick and wounded, both civilians and soldiers. The roads soon became crowded with people leaving home and possessions to flee eastwards. Early in September a large transport of evacuees from Poznań was travelling towards Warsaw and, as the train approached Szmanów station, a kilometre from the friary, it was bombed. The friars ran to solace the wounded and dying. On 7 September bombs were dropped on Niepokalanów and the neighbourhood but little damage was done.

The Polish army was badly deployed and ill-equipped to face Germany's military might and within days of the invasion the Polish forces were retreating to the Vistula and the garrison of Warsaw was preparing for a siege. On 17 September the Red Army crossed Poland's eastern frontier. It was a blow in the back which sealed the country's fate for there were no significant Polish reserves to meet the new invader. On the same day the Polish Government and High Command left for Romania. Hitler was determined that Warsaw should be captured before he had to negotiate a settlement with the Russians and he ordered that the Polish capital should be in German hands by the end of the month.

During the siege of Warsaw, Father Kolbe held constant prayers for the beleagured city and its defenders. His chasuble bore the words 'Regina Poloniae, ora pro nobis', Queen of Poland, pray for us.

The first of the Community was arrested some three

hundred kilometres from Warsaw near the seaport of Gdynia in the north. He was Brother Cornelius Maria Władysław who joined Niepokalanów in 1932 as a young seminarian, and made his final vows before Father Kolbe. He is still there today after serving five years and eight months in concentration camps. He is a man of singular stoicism filled with the Franciscan quality of happiness, a delicate gaiety: his mobile face reveals his every emotion: his deep-throated laugh shakes his square shoulders: his warm brown eyes show affection, and his friends are legion. His pen-friends alone now number two hundred all over the world. It was loyalty to friends which saved him from the gas chambers on one out of three occasions when he escaped death.

Brother Cornelius (Korneli to his friends) was arrested on 14 September 1939 while engaged on administrative affairs of the Niepokalanów Press. He was in the friary when he heard the shouts of German soldiers. 'I wanted to go to Mass but bayonets were directed towards me. They searched me and identified me as a soldier because of my short hair, and I was told I was sure to be shot. Everyone over eighteen had to go with them.' A high-ranking officer who came from Gdynia did not want to shoot in the presence of others. He decided to take them to a nearby wood for the purpose but suddenly it occurred to him to ask his subordinate why the men were to be shot. There was no reason. This did not stop many atrocities but halted this one.

After a fortnight Brother Cornelius was again told he was to be shot but the confusion of two names saved him. He variously used his religious name of Cornelius and his family name of Władysław. 'When they found I was one and the same person I was put in a penal company which meant execution next day. But the next morning other German officers came with record books in which I was registered as Władysław and they were looking for Cornelius.' Brother Cornelius said with his hearty laugh, 'They recognized me as another person. I received a blue card but didn't know its significance. Those given red cards were sent to be shot –

82

1. Maksymilian Kolbe

2. Maksymilian as a young friar. *(top left)*

3. Brother Zeno Zebrowski with one of the many Japanese children he befriended. *(top right)*

4. Maksymilian's mother, Marianna, in 1941. *(bottom right)*

5. Franciszek Gajowniczek, prisoner no. 5659, for whom Fr Kolbe gave his life in 1941.

6. Franciszek Gajowniczek and his wife, Helena, in 1981.

7. The Beatification of Maksymilian Maria Kolbe in Rome, 17 October 1971. From left to right: Cardinal Stefan Wyszyński, former Polish Primate, Franciszek Gajowniczek, Pope Paul VI, Cardinal Karol Wojtyła, Archbishop of Cracow (Pope John Paul II). *(below)*

8. Sculpture of Maksymilian Kolbe in Nowa Huta Church, Cracow. *(left)*

9. Detail of sculpture in Nowa Huta Church. *(top right)*

10. The Archbishop of Canterbury, Dr Robert Runcie, Pope John Paul II and Metropolitan Anthony of Sourozh praying in the Chapel of Saints and Martyrs of our own time in Canterbury Cathedral among whom Fr Kolbe is included. May 1982. *(bottom right)*

there were professors, priests, civic heads among the group – only six of us out of one hundred and fifty had blue.'

It was on the third occasion that his devotion to friends saved him. The gauleiter told them a transport of prisoners were to be released and his name was among them. Brother Cornelius recalls in his colourful English, 'I could not take a step forward. I wanted to stay with my comrades.' The party heading for freedom were gassed.

In his years in the camp every day was full of danger. A particularly vile practice was to offer 'leave' as a reward for shooting a Pole who was trying to escape. Cornelius set himself a tough mental discipline, to learn foreign languages. The daily target he gave himself was two hundred new words. Korneli now knows German, French, English, Latin, Italian and Esperanto. 'I was lucky,' he said, 'I was able to borrow books and I loved boys' adventure tales about the Indians.' He was often asked by prisoners and guards why he studied so hard. What was the use of learning languages today when tomorrow he would go to the crematorium? Brother Cornelius told them, 'I will not go there.' He always believed he would survive. On 29 April 1945 at 6.00 p.m. he was released by the Americans who reached Dachau Concentration Camp in Bavaria, West Germany.

At 10.00 a.m. on 19 September 1939 German motor-cycle troops roared up to the lodge gates at Niepokalanów. Father Kolbe summoned all the brothers by bell. The Germans wanted him to call a roll and give them names of all those who had left the friary and their whereabouts. The roll was not called but all the brothers were ordered to prepare to leave at once. Brother Hieronim, who is still with the Community in Poland, told the Germans that there were wounded Polish soldiers in the infirmary and someone had to care for them. Two brothers were allowed to stay. The friars begged Father Kolbe to remain but he refused. Then the brothers were marched to the main road escorted by armed Germans. Their Guardian, clasping his walking stick, which the Germans later confiscated despite his quiet protest that he was ill, urged them 'Take courage, my children. We're going on a mission and our fare is paid. Isn't that a stroke of luck!' The friars were to be interned as a precaution against the Community helping the Polish forces. Maksymilian had cautioned the brothers not to join the 'Underground' movement: there were many courageous men and women involved in the 'Resistance'; they were knights in another militia, trained to fight other battles.

The friars were driven in trucks to Rawa Mazowiecka, seventy kilometres south west of Warsaw, where they spent the night locked in the Church of the Passionist Fathers. After much entreaty women in the neighbourhood persuaded the Germans to allow them to bring food. The next day the brothers were driven to Częstochowa, and the steeple of the monastery at Jasna Góra, where the Black Madonna has been enshrined for six hundred years, seemed to beckon encouragement to them from Bright Mountain across the uncertain autumn mists. Once again local people seeing friars in the hands of Germans, rushed to offer food. At first the soldiers did not object but then refused their gifts. Undeterred, the people threw bread and cake and fruit; some whispered plans for escaping and offered civilian clothes. The Germans drove the brothers, touched by such solicitude, to the station and the journey was continued by cattle trucks. First they stayed for several days at Lamsdorf (called Lambinowice today) in Silesia, which was a camp for prisoners of war. Then they were taken to Amtitz (now known as Gębice) which is five hundred kilometres from Warsaw and near the German frontier. The place was not then a concentration camp but the friars were ill-treated, poorly fed, deprived of warmth and any privacy. There were huge military tents and the Franciscans were put in one for three hundred. Among the internees there was thieving and quarrelling; most were hungry, some were dying. Father Kolbe moved among them, giving comfort and distributing his 'bullets', the miraculous medals with which he had filled the capacious pockets of his habit.

As for the brothers, Maksymilian's presence was their consolation and he would encourage them gently, 'Courage, my children . . . let us learn how to profit from suffering . . . the end is in sight.' He told them, 'When suffering is remote, we are willing to do everything. Now that it's here let us accept it and bear it willingly . . .' With his intuition of yet worse trials ahead he suggested tentatively that they make a contract with the Virgin, to this end: 'I am willing to remain forgotten, comfortless, scorned and friendless in this camp, even though others return home. I am willing to die on this hard ground, in the company of these frigid hearts, and to be buried in that cemetery in the forest, if it is your will.' If they made such a commitment, even if they were freed, they would have earned the same merit as if they had actually endured it all.

Brother Hieronim recalls the pinching cold at Amtitz. When they had been taken so abruptly from the 'City' they thought optimistically that they would soon return. Some of the brothers had not worn socks. They had to sleep on the ground on straw, and there were mice. Roll-call was a trial of endurance for they had to stand for one or two hours both morning and night. Although Mass was forbidden, Father Kolbe heard confessions and gave many homilies which drew prisoners from all over the camp. It was forbidden to leave your own tent but the Germans did not enforce this rule rigidly. The Franciscans were fortunate in the camp overseers. The 'Gruppenführer' was Sergeant Sturn, a Berliner, and a Protestant; and the commander of the region, Lieutenant Zalewski, a German Catholic with a Polish mother. The friars fashioned a beautiful statue of the Virgin from clay, and more practically, they made themselves beds from planks. At first they drank their soup from tins for they had no utensils and then they carved some wooden spoons. The prison food did little to sustain stamina; their lot was bread and soup in which vegetable parings floated parsimoniously.

In spite of heavy air and artillery bombardment Warsaw held out until 28 September when the commander of the garrison signed the instrument of surrender and the Germans

85

rang church bells in rejoicing. Poland had been overrun in less than a month but the Poles refused to accept defeat. One day before the capitulation of the capital, the precursor of Poland's valiant Home Army (AK) was formed in Warsaw, and 'underground' activity increased. The first copies of a clandestine newspaper, *Poland Lives*, appeared in the capital. About this time a hundred Jews were released from Amtitz. They left exulting although to unknown destinations in Poland, and with their heads shaved in the sign of a cross.

On 9 November the Franciscans believed that they too were to be freed. German soldiers took them to the station and they boarded a train northwards. As they sang an ancient faithful hymn the winter sun shone bravely but perfunctorily. Their beloved 'City' was not their destination, but another prison at Schildberg (today called Ostrzeszów) near Kalisz, Poznań. Armed soldiers awaited them at the station and forced them to run to the camp in the secondary school of the Salesian Fathers which the Germans had requisitioned. The friars were housed in the cellars and the Commandant put them to work in the kitchens because some other prisoners stole. The prison held men from all over Poland caught in *łapanka* – random street 'round-ups'. Later in the war those rounded up in this way were sent to Germany to work, but at this time they were interned to ensure that they did not act against the German forces. There were many intellectuals among the internees and Maksymilian was able to organize readings and seminars which helped men's minds to vault the prison walls. They slept on the floor without blankets and food was scanty. The generosity of the local people was a godsend to the near-starving men. As soon as neighbours learned that the new prisoners were from Niepokalanów, they hurried to offer help for many were subscribers to the 'City's' publications.

A clever scheme was put into operation with the help of the Polish Red Cross. The Ostrzeszowians collected food, clothes and drugs and left them at the surgeries of the local doctor and dentist. The prisoners could get passes to go into

86

town for medical or dental care. They were escorted by a soldier intent on buying schnapps in the shops, while the prisoners had 'treatment'. They never tried to run away or the doctor would have been punished for his negligence. Local benefactors also managed to enrol the help of a camp carpenter and one of the German sentries in smuggling food. Before long the camp authorities became suspicious that so many prisoners needed to consult the doctor and they cut down on passes. Every day then two of the prisoners, accompanied by German guards, would wheel a hand-drawn cart into town to beg for food. Often one of the Franciscans, Brother Cyprian, would go with them and manage surreptitiously to hand out names of some of the internees to the townspeople, for food parcels handed into the camp office had to be addressed to individuals.

A week after the Franciscans arrived at Ostrzeszów, Hans Mulzer, a reserve lieutenant in the German divisions of the Border Guard, became camp commandant. Brother Hieronim describes him, 'He looked like Himmler but he was a noble man and kind to us, sharing our troubles.' On one occasion Maksymilian asked Lieutenant Mulzer if he would allow two of the interned fathers to celebrate Mass in the town. Hans Mulzer appeared nonplussed, angry even; the friars asked too much, he had already indulged them too far. Maksymilian felt conscience-stricken that he had upset the Commandant because he had shown them much consideration. He wondered if he should ask his pardon, and told his brothers that he would pass his fingers over the rosary and if they stopped on a number that could be divided by two it was a sign that it was God's will that he sought forgiveness from the German. Some may have thought he acted superstitiously rather than as a true religious, but he told them, 'If we don't know what to do, our conscience has a ready answer. There is no Superior to tell us and our fellow-prisoners cannot advise us. We can see God's will in this way.' So Father Kolbe sought the Commandant to make amends, but he brushed the apology aside; it was already forgotten, he said. Hans Mulzer tried to ease the stay of the friars as best he could. For weeks they had sorely felt the lack of spiritual comfort and early in December he arranged for the local priest to bring them Holy Communion.

Father Kolbe had predicted to the brothers that they would be released on the Feast Day of the Immaculate Conception and on the evening of 7 December they were told they would leave the next day. When dusk had fallen Hans Mulzer went himself to fetch the priest to give them Holy Communion. They were thankful to him for this privilege for which he risked demotion and disgrace. He also decided to have his photograph taken with the Franciscans before they left, and in doing so he ran the risk of years of imprisonment for fraternizing, which was forbidden.

Maksymilian had a rare gift for friendship, even with his captors. He drew a sketch map showing the whereabouts of Niepokalanów and Hans Mulzer promised he would visit the Community after the war. Maksymilian also took a 'miraculous medal' from the small purse he carried in his habit and asked the German officer to take it 'for remembrance'. It was this gift which made Mulzer reveal his priesthood. At first he said, 'I cannot take it; I am not only a German soldier, officer and commandant of the camp but I am also a Protestant minister and we do not have such admiration for the Virgin Mary as you do.' Yet he did accept the little holy medallion.

In the afternoon of 8 December 1939 the Franciscans were escorted by German soldiers to Ostrzeszów station, the local people lining the road to bid them godspeed. On the homeward journey there were many delays and the brothers worried lest they should be interned again in some transit camp.

They spent the night in the train and arrived in Warsaw the next morning. The friars found parts of the city in ruins. Rubble was being cleared by Poles and Jews who wore yellow stripes on their sleeves. Everywhere Germans paraded, arrogant in victory. They made their way to the Franciscan cloisters which still stood, a stoical refuge in Zakroczymska Street. Their brothers had told them that the Germans had arrested

88

many priests in an attempt to terrorize the ordinary people. Father Kolbe celebrated Mass, assisted by his friars, before leaving for Niepokalanów. Everywhere they were greeted like closest friends by neighbours. In their three months' absence the friary had been robbed and vandalized, but not destroyed. Statues and pictures had been desecrated and broken, much of their expensive modern equipment removed. Maksymilian remained serene and said, 'Mary Immaculate has given us all, she takes all back. Let us accept with love all the crosses.' As usual he was asking a lot from the brothers – love without limits – because five days after their return German soldiers hauled away the wood the friars had amassed to build a church. The friars begged Father Kolbe not to stay in Niepokalów, but to take refuge in another friary, for they did not believe that the German authorities would leave him in peace. He was touched by their concern, but said that his place was with them. He started to repair the damage, placing a new column with a statue of the Virgin at the entrance to the 'City'. He also introduced Perpetual Adoration so that the brothers, turn by turn, prayed continuously, throughout the day. Maksymilian's intentions were to strengthen the spiritual life of the friars and increase their charitable work. He interceded successfully with the German authorities for the return of many of the Community. He wanted to safeguard their vocation and save them from concentration camps. The authorities allowed the friars back in force because there was much work. The 'City' had itself become a vast camp for refugees, deportees, political prisoners, and Jews.

CHAPTER EIGHT

In the Primitive Rule of Francis approved by Pope Innocent III, the early followers of the saint were begged '. . . to be humble and charitable, and *to perform manual labour*'. 'I work with my hands', Francis wrote in his Testament, 'It is my earnest desire that all the brethren should work at a trade in conformity with honesty.' With the evolution of the Order since medieval times, to labour with your hands is no longer prescribed. Yet Francis' words must have spoken to the friars across the breadth of seven centuries, as if he were working at their side, when the publishing house of Kolbe's Militia was converted into war-time workshops. The print shops were expanded and the brothers turned their hands to the manufacture and repair of agricultural machinery. There were also workshops for watch repairs, bicycle repairs, a photographic 'shop', cobbler, bakery, and, by order of the Germans, a district dairy. The Voluntary Fire Brigade operated widely and the friars ran a first-aid station. The Germans' sufferance of Niepokalanów owed much to its usefulness. It had become like a small town with its population cramped, hungry and fearful, bereft of homes and livelihood.

Soon after the Franciscans returned, the first transports of deportees from northern and western regions of Poland arrived at the friary. In October Hitler had annexed these regions to create two new districts of Germany, the Reichsgau Danzig and the Reichsgau Wartheland, and for Polish territory in central and southern Poland he established a German administration called the Government-General. The annexed areas included Polish Pomerania, Upper Silesia, the Dąbrowa basin, part of the province of Lódź and the Suwałki Salient, with a total population of more than ten millions. These lands were to be completely Germanized and their Polish character erased. The Polish inhabitants whom the Germans considered to be a threat to the Reich, or unfit for Germanization, were to be deported either to the Government-General or to Germany for ultimate extermination. This was most of them.

About 3,000 Poles, including 1,500 Jews, were abandoned by the Germans at Niepokalanów where Maksymilian and his brothers surrounded them with illimitable love and practical concern. Before the German authorities arranged any pittance of food for them, Father Kolbe appealed to neighbours who shared their own, and opened their doors to the homeless. The refugees tried to help themselves. They organized a form of self-government, a management committee with representatives of different towns, and individuals who assumed specific responsibilities. These included maintaining the discipline of the group, food supplies, clerical work, and finding new homes in the capital and its environs, and among the neighbours of Niepokalanów.

On Christmas Eve 1939 a solemn Midnight Mass was celebrated and ardent prayers offered. The homeless Poles were given the solace of the sacraments and sang traditional carols which bestowed the balm of the familiar. But it was not all prayers and piety. Remarkably, the friars who had only just been freed from internment themselves to go home to a devastated friary, were able with childlike enthusiasm to conjure Christmas magic for all in the shape of confections from the bakery. No one was left out, and St Nicholas gave each child a gift as well as little bags of sweets. Maksymilian knew intuitively that it would be the last Christmas for many whom the friary was sheltering. The friars showed a caressing tenderness to the old, the young, and the Jews, who were given their own celebration on New Year's Day, a special day in their calendar. The fact that it was not the actual Jewish New Year, Rosh Hashanah – this falls on the 1st of Tishri, the name of a month that comes partly in September and partly in October – counted for nothing.

It was the thoughtfulness of the Franciscans which moved the Jews near to tears. They came from many occupations: among them were craftsmen, shopkeepers, writers, doctors, lawyers. In their brief sojourn with the charitable brothers they seemed to sense impending tragedy, but it is recorded by one of the brothers, Juwentyn Młodozeniec, that the Jews preserved a mental poise and inner peace which was a gleaming example. Before they left they asked that a special Mass of Thanksgiving be celebrated to praise God for his protection over them and Niepokalanów. They promised to write after the war but ominously no letters were received; such silence was self-explanatory.

Soon after the Jews and other deportees had left, another transport of some 1500 Pomeranians arrived early in April. It was 1940 when German might seemed invincible, and on Adolf Hitler's birthday, 20 April, the forlorn and disinherited people were ordered to decorate the buildings and display a sign proclaiming, 'Eine Welt, Ein Volk, Ein Führer!' – One World, one Nation, one Leader. The Pomeranians left Niepokalanów in July. Some settled in the province of the Government-General: others were sent in closed trucks for forced labour in Germany or to concentration camps.

There soon arose an urgent need to nurse the wounded and Father Kolbe opened a health care centre in Niepokalanów at the request of the Polish Red Cross (PCK) of the Sochaczew District. During the war German units were often stationed at Niepokalanów and Maksymilian would include the German soldiers in his ministrations, especially the sick among them. German officials, too, frequently came to oversee the management of the dairy and workshops. They were escorted by Maksymilian himself who would often take them into the chapel where the brothers prayed ceaselessly, succeeding each other day and night. 'This is the most important work at Niepokalanów', he would tell the German officers in his soft voice, and he would give them 'miraculous medals'.

Despite the commonplace demands of everyday living at Niepokalanów in war time, the spiritual dimension was never neglected. The novitiate was restarted for clerics and brothers who studied in secret. Lessons were given to secondary school standard. This was illegal – all education except rudimentary primary teaching went 'underground' – but when questioned the friars feigned naivety; this was not a school but a seminary and its purpose was religious instruction, they said. On 8 December 1940 twenty-two young men made their perpetual vows. The continuation and expansion of Niepokalanów was regarded by many as miraculous. Other Franciscan friaries had been closed by the German authorities and Maksymilian had accepted the displaced friars. He wrote to many of his own brethren who could not return because of boundary difficulties and to others who had helped found the Japanese 'Garden of the Immaculate'. His letters as always were short, their purpose to encourage the brothers in constancy and courage.

Maksymilian had often discussed with his brothers how best to channel the work of the Community upon their release from internment, and all agreed that the gates of the friary must be opened wide to the homeless and the casualties of war. He now resolved to try to resume publication of *The Knight of the Immaculate*, and characteristically wasted no time. In December 1939 he took a letter to the Subprefecture in Sochaczew asking for permission. He told the authorities that *The Knight* had been published in three languages while the aims of the Militia had been published in thirteen. 'We hope in time to publish in every language', he wrote, '. . . politics have never entered our goals, nor ever will, as the enclosed statutes prove.' He added, 'For these statutes I am willing to sacrifice my life at any time.' He also pressed his cause with the Board of People's Education and Propaganda in Warsaw, where the director, Dr Kurt Grundmann, had been a professor of German at Warsaw University before the war. A written permit followed from the office of the Governor General in Cracow. The friary's printing machines were still sealed with lead, so Maksymilian went to the Gestapo in Warsaw to show the authorization: not only did they refuse to free the machines but confiscated the permit. Yet Maksymilian persisted in his appeals to publish; he saw it as an important gesture to raise the spirits of his readers; and on 21 November he received permission from the Board of People's Education and Propaganda in Warsaw for a single edition to be circulated only in the Warsaw district. Most of the 120,000 copies of the edition, labelled optimistically by Maksymilian as a bi-monthly, December 1940 – January 1941, which suggested further editions would follow, were delivered by hand. This was surer than entrusting them to the post. In the paper Maksymilian wrote, 'No one in the world can alter truth; find it, and be its servant . . . Not even the most powerful propaganda machine in the world can change truth. The real conflict is an inner conflict. Beyond armies of occupation, unrestrained passions and the hecatombs of extermination camps, there are two irreconcilable enemies in the depth of every soul: good and evil, sin and love. And what use are the victories on the battlefield if we are defeated in our innermost personal selves?'

One of the Franciscans, Father John Burdyszek, who brought The Crusade to England in 1952, at once saw its strength. 'It was like the echo of Christ's words, "Do not fear, I am with you."' Many letters in the edition blazoned brave expressions of Polish patriotism, and no doubt attracted the disapproval of the Germans. Maksymilian hoped to continue in print and on 24 January 1941 he wrote to his mother, 'We are trying to get a permit for the February edition of *The Knight* . . . We need prayers desperately.' But his subsequent petitions were turned down peremptorily.

It was probably the Catholic daily, *Maly Dziennik* (Little Daily), first published at Niepokalanów on 27 May 1935, which most angered the Germans. It was a lively and assertive newspaper concerned equally with secular and religious affairs. In common with other Polish newspapers it had published articles which criticized the Third Reich, who suppressed it upon the outbreak of war, and thus Kolbe's activities came under scrutiny and suspicion.

Maksymilian did not need the gifts of prophecy to realize that his future was precarious; his one wish was to make his brothers fearless apostles of the Immaculate, radiating Franciscan love to neighbours. He was adamant that he would not sign the Volkslist which meant renouncing Polish nationality to acknowledge German citizenship. The military police pressed him to sign for his name suggested German origins. Maksymilian declared that he felt a true Pole and that his roots were Polish. In fact his great-grandfather came from Moravia with a group of unemployed Czechs, and in the north of Czechoslovakia today the name of Kolbe is common. Those who did sign the Volkslist saved themselves from deportation, or worse, the concentration camps: it was a safety net. Understandably many decided in favour of claiming German descent in these cruel circumstances. In German Silesia there were many Poles with Polish names who became Germanized; it was a protracted and painful process completed by Nazi terror. Yet as the war developed and the Nazis were shown in their true and terrible light, more and more Volksdeutschen began to realize that they had been wrong to be so coerced for they could own to nothing in common with the Germans. Many expiated their weakness in signing by subsequent heroic work in the 'Resistance', and in smuggling relief to the victims of the camps.

When Maksymilian was arrested on 17 February 1941 it was as a journalist and publisher who was not afraid to print the truth as he saw it, and as one of the country's condemned 'intellectuals'. Such a description of the gentle priest, whose words swayed the mass of Polish people by their directness and simplicity, would amaze some of his critics who saw him as unsophisticated and naive, and found his papers lacking intellectual depth. But priests came second to Jews in Hitler's hate-list. Each transport to Auschwitz concerntration camp was greeted by the SS officer in charge of new prisoners with the words; 'If there are Jews in the transport, they cannot live more than two weeks, if there are priests, they may live one month, the rest three months.'

Maksymilian received a warning of his impending arrest. It was believed to have come from a young Polish woman from Poznań who had been deported from her home and billeted at Niepokalanów. Later she was made to work as a secretary at Gestapo headquarters in Aleje Szucha in Warsaw. She was fluent in German and the Gestapo reasoned that she would be useful to them. For her part she thought that she might be able to help her friends by alerting them to danger. She had become fond of the Franciscan Fathers who had given her help and reassurance as a refugee, and she knew about the plans of the secret police to arrest Father Kolbe. A warning arrived for him in the form of an enigmatic 'bill' so that it did not arouse suspicion in the post. It appeared that three men questioned and possibly tortured at Gestapo headquarters laid charges against Father Kolbe which gave them a superficial pretext for his arrest. There are uncertainties about who made these accusations. One suspect was a sergeant in the Polish Army, believed to be a spy. He was made an administrator of the estate of Prince Drucki-Lubecki as a reward. The palace and grounds near Niepokalanów had been requisitioned for the hospitality of German governors. There was also the unlikely rumour that one of the Franciscans had denounced Father Kolbe, and after the war the Community questioned this brother. He denied it, and told them that the statement he gave the Gestapo was taken down in German which he did not understand. He signed it but perhaps it had been fabricated and so he had been tricked. It is empty speculation because it was apparent that Kolbe was to be persecuted anyway, as a man who had wielded too much influence through his Militia and printing presses. Such leaders of men must be removed before the Poles became slaves.

Maksymilian made no attempt to avoid arrest because he knew the stratagem of the Nazis. If a wanted person was missing, his family or friends were taken in his place, and he did not intend that the brothers should suffer for him.

Often in those last days he asked Brother Arnold, his official secretary, and Brother Karol Rufin, his personal secretary, to come to his room and listen to his exposition on the relationship of the Holy Trinity to the Immaculate, for he knew that not all of the brothers would understand what he wanted to say. Brother Rufin occupied the adjoining cell and, as a close friend, he was told that he could always visit him without knocking. Shortly before Father Kolbe was arrested, Brother Rufin came to his cell unexpectedly and later observed, 'It seemed as if he had been visited by some bad spirit.' He looked tense, and appeared fatigued, preoccupied; and he was sprinkling holy water.

On 16 February, the eve of his arrest, Maksymilian went to the cells of the oldest of the brothers and said simply that he would like to take supper with them. This was not his custom and the friars were surprised and pleased. It was not a feast but it had the air of a special and solemn occasion. Five brothers shared the small cake which Father Kolbe brought, and tea was made from apple peelings. The brothers who celebrated this Last Supper included those who had worked on the paper in the early days at Grodno. Father Kolbe spoke a long time and he dwelt especially on his most beloved theme, the relationship of the Holy Trinity to the Virgin Mary. He repeated several times that it is difficult to understand such concepts. 'It is a grace so one has to pray on one's knees to understand this holy secret.' The brothers were much impressed by him on that day. He did not tell them of the warning he had received: his visit had been unusual but they had not suspected that this was his leavetaking.

On Maksymilian's last day at Niepokalanów, he aroused Brother Rufin at 4.00 a.m., an hour earlier than the friars usually rose. Father Kolbe was dressed in his best habit, similar to his everyday one but unpatched and therefore kept for Holy Days and Feast Days. The brother was surprised to see him because he was not ill, though scrupulous in sick-visiting: in retrospect Rufin knew that he wished to say goodbye. They talked particularly about the relationship of the

97

Immaculate to the Trinity. Brother Rufin said, 'He was quiet and sober and it seemed as if he had tears in his eyes.'

After Mass and breakfast he told Brother Rufin he wanted to dictate an article on the theme of the Trinity and the Virgin Mary, but Brother Arnold took the dictation because Brother Rufin had many letters to answer. Father Kolbe had for several years been preparing material for a profound book upon this theme but recently work on the manuscript could only be fragmentary because war-work made urgent demands on time. His thesis was that Mary was the chief visible manifestation of the presence of the Holy Spirit in the Church and the universal instrument of the Spirit's mission to unite all men to Christ. His Marian theology was a precursor of the keystone of Vatican II, the Constitution on the Church, *Lumen Gentium*. This elucidated the role Mary plays in the Church, a privileged role, even though it remains in total subordination to that of Christ. In the moving pages Father Kolbe wrote hours before his second and final arrest he declared that Mary was 'the spouse, handmaid and sanctuary of the Holy Spirit'.

That morning, 17 February, he had finished the chapter at about 9.30 a.m. when the telephone rang. It was the Gatekeeper to tell Father Kolbe that the Gestapo were asking to see him. Brother Arnold had the impression that Father Kolbe had been expecting them. He was working until the last minute; it was as if he wanted to impress on the brothers how he wished them to persevere in their labours. He remained calm and went to meet them. Some brothers hauling lumber on a cart to the sawmill were obstructing their way and Maksymilian told them, 'Wait, my children. Allow the gentlemen to pass.' He saluted them first, with the words, 'Praised be Jesus Christ.' Then he offered the Germans some coffee which they refused, and he showed them around the friary.

Brother Cherubin, one of the firemen, was in the workshops when Father Kolbe came in with the Gestapo. 'I thought that they were just visitors because Father Kolbe was quite at ease. He bowed his head to friars busy in the workshop and they thought this was merely a courtesy on his part; they didn't construe it as a last farewell.'

The Germans asked, not for the first time, if Niepokalanów ran a school, which was forbidden, and Father Kolbe explained patiently, if with deliberate obtuseness, that it was not an educational establishment but a seminary to train clerics. They looked around the printing works and were surprised to see that a brother was setting some agricultural news in German. They asked for a list of the friars who had left the monastery of their own free will as if they were looking for something against Kolbe. They toured the kitchens and were amazed by the meagre portions in preparation. When their inspection was finished, Father Kolbe was arrested together with four other priests who were connected with publishing. They were Father Justin Nazim, Father Pius Bartosik, Father Urban Cieślak, and Father Antoni Bajewski (Fathers Bartosik and Bajewski died at Auschwitz in 1941; the other two survived the camp). Brother Rufin sent to the kitchens for bread to take on the journey because they had had a lean breakfast. The Gestapo told Father Kolbe he would return, but he knew this was false: a year earlier he had predicted that he would not survive the war and he repeated this prophecy at many conferences. Turning to his closest brethren, he said serenely, 'The Immaculate will look after you.' He took a small bag for it was his way to travel light, and one of the brothers fetched his cloak. The day was cloudy and frosty. Father Kolbe asked for a few moments to appoint his successor, choosing Father George Wierdak as Guardian and Father Florian Koziura as his assistant.

At midday the Community gathered to eat in the refectory and Father Florian rang a bell to summon attention. Sombrely he told them that Father Kolbe had just been arrested. Some of the brothers were in tears. Brother Cherubin recalled that in olden times there were religious orders whose duties were to pray for prisoners, but he thought that they should offer their lives for Father Kolbe. He spoke about his plan to Father Florian who allowed him to collect signatures of those prepared to offer themselves as hostages. Many of the friars declared they would sign 'with both hands', but there were some who hesitated, and many more were occupied outside the friary. He collected twenty signatures and Father Florian took the petition to the Gestapo who could not begin to comprehend the spirit of self-sacrifice which had prompted it. It was inconceivable that Father Kolbe would have agreed to such an exchange because he never allowed himself the smallest privilege. But their offer was refused for the Germans were bent on destroying the Polish leadership and dividing Church and State. When asked why the Germans were murdering Polish priests, Conrad Henlein, Governor Frank's deputy, replied in these words, 'Since in Poland, the Church and the nation are one, we must split this union. That's why we strike once at the Church and once at the nation to destroy you.'

The Community did not offer a high bribe to the Germans for the return of their beloved Guardian because they were worldly-wise enough to be aware of the cynical cruelties practised by the Nazis. Often they would release a prisoner in exchange for a large sum of money and within a short time would re-arrest him.

Maksymilian and the four other priests were taken first to Pawiak in Warsaw, which was the investigative prison of the Secret Police during the Occupation. During the war 100,000 were brought to these cells of whom 60,000 were sent to concentration camps. They included those whom the Nazis arrested in their homes or in 'łapanka', prisoners of war, escapees and airmen shot down over Polish territory. (On 30 July 1944 the Nazis evacuated some of the prisoners, shot the rest and blew up the buildings. The vaults and prison yard have been reconstructed and now a museum stands on the site. An obelisk hewn in granite bears reliefs symbolizing captivity, struggle and freedom.)

Father Kolbe's trials began at once. Before he was given prison clothes he wore his habit and the crucifix on his rosary so enraged one of the SS gaolers that he tried to make Maksymilian renounce his beliefs by beating him with his fists and tearing the Franciscan beads from him. Kolbe remained steadfast and encouraged the prisoners to pray as a means of strength. Around this time he wrote to the Community, 'Let all the brothers pray much, work conscientiously without worry, because nothing can happen without God's knowledge and will . . .'

A fellow prisoner, Edward Gniadek, later testified to Kolbe's conduct in Pawiak. 'His calm presence and conversation had a great effect on improving my nervous condition for I was living under the fear that I would be summoned for questioning or sent to a camp.' He witnessed the incident in which the SS guard assaulted Father Kolbe and confirmed, 'He did not lose his control for a moment; I didn't notice any nervousness and after the Gestapo had left he said to me, "Don't get upset, you have your own troubles enough. Don't be sorry for me, it's all for the Immaculate." He said it quietly, as if nothing had happened.' Edward Gniadek then lost touch with Father Kolbe who was taken to hospital with chest trouble. Later when in Dachau concentration camp Gniadek heard about Kolbe's death at Auschwitz. 'I was not surprised,' he said, 'I knew he was a man capable of such heroism.'

In testaments collected at Niepokalanów after the war, a fellow professor and priest told how he and Kolbe confessed to each other in the privacy of the prison library. Father Kolbe worked in the library among young people from the intelligentsia of Warsaw who held him in high regard.

Another Pawiak prisoner, Jan Jakub Szegidewicz, a Muslim of Tartar origin, was sent once to Gestapo headquarters for questioning and was badly beaten. When he returned Father Kolbe tried to console him. 'When he learned that I was of another religion he showed great insight and delicacy. He didn't try to force his religious beliefs on me. He asked me about other Tartars in Poland, about national and

101

religious customs and our holy days. He tried to create an atmosphere of optimism and belief in survival.'

Szegidewicz also related how two prisoners were brought to Pawiak from Auschwitz and told them about the camp. 'Father Kolbe asked how priests were treated in Auschwitz but we couldn't believe these two prisoners. It seemed to us this information could not be true.' On 28 May Father Kolbe was taken to Auschwitz in a transport of three hundred. As the wagons began to move the soft underswell of a hymn to the Virgin was heard. It was Maksymilian Kolbe leading the singing and the 'crescendo' became an august anthem of praise.

CHAPTER NINE

Peaceful country roads with little wayside altars thread through villages of wood and thatched cottages to Oświęcim in the Province of Cracow in the south of Poland. Old women, shouldering hoes like muskets, are helped by children to weed the fields. It's a gentle approach to an innocuous-sounding place at the union of the Vistula and Sota rivers. Before the war it was a small and rather disagreeable town, poorly industralized, boggy and polluted, in a flat dispiriting landscape. It was soon to attract infamous and worldwide notoriety as the site selected by Heinrich Himmler, head of the SS, for the biggest crematorium in the world. When the Germans annexed this land in 1939, they called the place Auschwitz, and the camp complex became known collectively by this name, a name to haunt the conscience of man. In four years four million people were to die here, for Auschwitz, as well as serving as a labour camp, was to become the largest extermination camp organized by the Nazis. Its first commandant was Rudolf Höss, son of a retired colonel. His father had longed to see the future commandant of Auschwitz take holy orders, and his upbringing at home had been strict and Roman Catholic in spirit.

Today Auschwitz is a 'Museum' – the word has cultural connotations inappropriate for a place of terror and torture – where sober pilgrims come to remember the dead and bring flowers from all over the world.

When Kolbe's transport arrived in May 1941, Auschwitz was a labour camp, yet also a death-camp because hundreds of thousands died under 'ordinary' working conditions. The war was going well for the Germans and the prisoners were expendable. They were all Poles for the first year apart from German criminals, 'on loan' from overcrowded prisons, who were the earliest 'trusties' used to help run the camp and allowed to bully their fellow-prisoners for twenty-four hours a day. New prisoners were issued with blue-and-white-striped serge pyjamas, soiled and second-hand, and bearing identifying triangles: red denoted political prisoners; yellow, Jewish; green, criminals; black, anti-socials; pink, homosexuals; and violet labelled Jehovah's Witnesses. Priests were not given an emblem and some concealed their calling for fear that the German criminals among the prisoners would kill them. The same risk was run by judges, prosecutors and policemen.

Maksymilian Kolbe made no secret of his profession as a man of God and servant of Mary and from the start he was vilified, although to make distinctions between degrees of sadism seems specious.

At the Admissions Block before the Gate, with its sardonic slogan *Arbeit Macht Frei* (Through Work to Freedom), names were forfeited for tattooed numbers and new prisoners had to repeat their numbers correctly in German else they were punished. Thus Poles who could not, or would not, speak German were punished from the outset. Maksymilian spoke good German and was spared this chastisement but his persecution was swift to follow. He was given the heaviest work in a kommando under 'Capo' Heinrich Krott (the word 'Capo' comes from the Italian for 'chief' and was used by Italian workmen making roads in southern Germany) who ordered the prisoners to move felled timber 'at the double'. They had to carry 70–80 kilogrammes of logs over rough ground. Kolbe often fell under the weight and was severely beaten, yet when fellow prisoners offered help he refused, for he feared they too would be punished. On one occasion Krott loaded him with double the usual number of logs and ordered him to run. Kolbe managed one or two steps, collapsed, and was promptly kicked in the face and stomach. The capo then instructed one of his burly henchmen to give the priest fifty lashes and after the beating Maksymilian was pushed into a hollow in the wood and left for dead. Under cover of night his friends returned to carry him to the camp hospital. Father Konrad Szweda, the camp nurse, said, 'he was beaten black and blue and was very feverish . . . but in my difficult moments he consoled *me*, raising my spirits. I owe a great deal to his motherly heart.' Father Kolbe rallied, and ignoring orders, heard confessions throughout the nights and cradled the dying and frightened as tenderly as any woman. His job, he saw plainly, was to minister to the needs of others and not to be ministered to. The camp was the place to practise the faith under the most appalling, or as he probably saw it, ideal circumstances: it was the crucible of affliction to fire Christian love.

Maksymilian wrote only one letter to his mother from Auschwitz, for, as he explained, he needed to help his fellow-prisoners with their letters home. They were allowed to send one letter a fortnight but written only in German. As customary his letter to Marianna (15 June 1941) was short and reassuring.

Dear Mother,
. . .I'm faring well. Be calm, Mother, and don't worry about me or my health. God is everywhere. He watches over all and everything with great love. . .

Despite orders and threats there were religious observances in Auschwitz but always conducted in secrecy. Kazimierz Smoleń, who is now director of Auschwitz Museum, was in the camp 'Underground' from its earliest days and confirms that there were Masses held surreptitiously in such places as a corner of the hospital, or the cellars of the X-ray unit. The communion host and wine were smuggled into the camp with the help of a conspiratorial organization by prisoners working outside the compound. Other former prisoners said communion wine sometimes came from 'Canada', the name symbolic of riches given to the huge store of loot taken from the Jews who were gassed, and that for sacramental bread Father

105

Kolbe sometimes used bread out of his ration saying, 'Take this, it is the bread of God . . .'

Prisoners recollected confessions made in the most extraordinary circumstances, hurriedly in corridors when awaiting interrogation, whispered while walking to work. Christ was a presence in the camp, and on the stone wall of a cell a prisoner had etched the likeness of Christ with his fingernails. German soldiers took photographs to send to their families and there is a picture of a prisoner decorated as Christ, wearing a wreath of thorns with soldiers taunting him, 'Let Christ help you now – the SS rule here.'

Many spoke of the will to survive inspired by Kolbe who found an extraordinary strength to minimize his own suffering. After a spell in the camp hospital he was moved to the invalids' block where he was exempt from work but received only half rations. He was not deterred from sharing even these. Hunger in Auschwitz was destroying more prisoners than any other torture except the gas chambers, and famine stalked the camp while Commandant Höss and his family feasted like kings in their grand house secluded in the compound, which his wife likened to 'an earthly paradise'. Not content with issuing starvation rations, the SS contrived wholesale robbery of the prisoners' food for their own kitchens. The whimsically named 'trusties' also stole their rations. In consequence a prisoner received on average 1500 calories a day – about a third of the number considered an indispensable 'norm'. Prison fare consisted of bread containing fifty per cent sawdust with a scraping of margarine; turnip soup for which they queued on their knees, and coffee concocted from herbs and grasses.

A fellow-prisoner and intellectual, who had met Kolbe before the war at a meeting of editors, met him again peeling potatoes at Auschwitz. He had been deeply impressed by him and recalled, 'At midday we usually had a plate of soup with turnips – the potatoes were stolen by the capos and cooks. Everyone was tired and hungry and looking forward to the so-called soup. Father Kolbe got his plate, crossed himself and began to eat. From another room a young prisoner approached him and asked rudely for the thin soup. Father gave it to him.' The observer commented, 'He is a second St Martin. In the conditions of the camp it was in truth a good deed. The instinct to survive would not allow anyone to give all his meal away.'

Maksymilian was able to marry spirituality with practicality. He refused several times to be taken to hospital asking that a younger man be treated in his place. Dr Rudolf Diem said his duty was to examine within an hour or two up to three hundred prisoners seeking medical aid. He rarely had time to see them all. 'When I suggested to Father Kolbe that he should come into hospital, he would single out a younger man and ask me to take him instead. I told him that there would be room for both of them but he would merely say, "Good, then please take the next man."' Dr Diem learnt that he was a priest and asked him if refusing to go to hospital made any sense in the camp when the fight for life was continual. Kolbe said shortly that everyone had an aim in life, going home to wife, sweetheart or mother, but he devoted his life to helping everybody and he believed that nothing would happen to him except by God's will.

Władysław Lewkowicz, another inmate, said that the longer Kolbe was in the camp the more prisoners sought his religious advice. Sometimes they gathered in a secretly appointed place and he talked to them; it was more a conversation than a sermon. He spoke often about the Immaculate (he always used that name for the Virgin) and her relationship with the Trinity. He proved that he was 'a good theologian' as well as a true comforter. Lewkowicz added, 'For me the later years in Auschwitz and in Buchenwald were not so hard to bear because Father Kolbe prepared me for all suffering and even death.' Zygmunt Kotodziejski, another prisoner, said it was difficult to speak to Father Kolbe because he was always surrounded by so many, among them well-known intellectuals, politicians, and radicals.

Another testimony came from Józef Stemler who first met

107

Kolbe in the spring of 1938 at a conference of the Association of Newspaper Editors. 'He proved to be an expert in the entire field of editorial work, although he seemed a little embarrassed that it was *he* who knew the answers to so many editorial problems'. His own daily *Maly Dziennik* (Little Daily) had become a challenge to long-established newspapers. 'There was nothing artificial in his behaviour, he was serious but happy and he had the smile of a youth – these qualities attracted many people to him.' Their next meeting was in Auschwitz. Stemler was repairing roads in the camp. He recalled an incident at the end of July that will always stay with him. 'I was coming back from the evening roll-call, half-dead from work and hunger, when I was ordered by an SS guard to go to the hospital to carry the dead bodies to the crematorium. I was not young but I had never before touched a corpse. The sight of the body of a young man, obviously tortured before death, made me nearly faint. Seeing my hesitation the SS man shouted at me, then I heard a calm voice, "Let's take him, brother." After we had taken out the bodies, read the prisoners' numbers to the SS men, and put them on a high heap of corpses waiting to be burnt, I was in despair. My companion pushed me gently towards the door and when I heard his quiet words "Requiescat in pace" I realized it was Father Kolbe.'

Stemler confessed to him, 'What I said was full of rebellion but nothing could shake his belief in the victory of good over evil; he insisted hatred could create nothing, only love gave creative power; and that these sufferings would not break us but strengthen us.'

Alexander Dziuba worked with Father Kolbe in the same kommando building roads, and told how the priest would meet some of the prisoners on Sundays out of sight of SS men and capos and tell them about the Polish and Japanese Niepokalanów. 'He said often "a man is a worm, the soul is important: you may lose everything, it doesn't matter; but if your soul is lost, you yourself are lost." His words gave us strength. There was some unusual spiritual power in him. I confessed to him on the camp street at night and I felt a sense of well-being just to be with him. He had his own secrets' – Dziuba guessed one – 'perhaps the Immaculate gave him some consolation and promised he would be in heaven.'

One of Poland's champion boxers before the war, Tadeusz Pietrzykowski, known as Teddy, a man not given to sentimentality, speaks of Kolbe's 'almost crazy courage'. This tribute comes from a man not lacking in the quality himself. He won two medals, one for bravery in the war and the second for his 'underground' work. While trying to escape to England to be a pilot he was caught on the boundaries of Yugoslavia and later sent to Auschwitz. He was one of the first to join the camp's Resistance movement, and for two years was assistant to Witold Pilecki who started it. A man of remarkable daring, Pilecki deliberately allowed himself to be caught in a street round-up in Warsaw to be sent to Auschwitz to organize the 'Underground'. Teddy said it was the aim of the Germans that human beings should cease to be human beings in the camp. 'Everybody was starving and a man is an egoist when he's starving and doesn't care what is going on; all he can think about is getting a bit of bread. It was not only the last sacrifice of Maksymilian Kolbe which was remarkable but his whole behaviour in the camp. He often offered himself to be beaten in place of someone else and he always shared his rations.'

Teddy was frequently able to earn a little more to eat by boxing. The Germans, apparently short of excitement, used to give him permission to fight some of the SS guards, and being a top-class sportsman, although much weaker than his usual condition, he did. They would bet on him and his prize would be extra bread which he distributed among friends. One piece he gave to Father Kolbe was stolen and Teddy began to beat the thief despite the priest's protests. Again he gave Kolbe the bread only to see it handed back to the thief. 'He had too great a heart', said Teddy, 'it was just against all reason.' Another day he was working in the fields where Kolbe was making fences when he saw him being beaten.

Teddy remonstrated with the capo, 'That SS man is obstructing the work.' The German agreed that he should hit the guard but Father Kolbe knelt before him and pleaded with him to stop. It was such an unusual scene that he supposed Kolbe was 'not a reasonable man'. Teddy was called as a witness against Commandant Höss after the war. He was also among the first to testify about Father Kolbe's behaviour to Brother Arnold, the priest's official secretary at Niepokalanów. Teddy told him simply, 'it was providence, what happened in the camp. He was a man selected by God – like our Pope.'

Father Kolbe never accepted food from other prisoners but one gift which he did take and treasure, was given him by the Polish artist Kościelniak, imprisoned at Auschwitz. Father Kolbe asked him to produce secretly a picture of Mary and the infant Jesus, so he drew it on a scrap of paper no larger than a postage stamp and Kolbe stuck it inside his belt.

The fortunes of war still favoured the Germans in the spring of 1941. Great Britain had won the Battle of Britain, but only just. Hitler had subjugated both Greece and Yugoslavia. America was still neutral and Soviet Russia not only kept out of the war but helped the Führer with huge supplies. The brutality in the concentration camps increased; more prisoners were murdered, driven on the electric wires, drowned in the latrines, starved and worked to death. The roll-calls were prolonged to increase the deaths, and when a prisoner escaped the invidious system of collective responsibility was operated. In retaliation for individual escapers men living in the same block were selected to die in a starvation bunker, and parents and wives, brothers and sisters, of the escaper were often arrested and brought to the camp. There were two kinds of escapers: some prisoners undertook special tasks for the 'Underground' and their escapes were prepared; the others were 'freelance'. All were condemned by the camp 'Underground' as 'extreme selfishness' in 1941 because of the brutal reprisals. Pilecki, the 'resistance' leader, wrote in his memoirs 'all escapes were "wild-cat" affairs for the time being and had nothing to do with our organization.'

Under the heat on a day at the end of July, men from Father Kolbe's Block stood on the camp street all day tortured by sun, hunger – their last 'meal' had been the previous evening – and fear. A prisoner had escaped from a farming kommando and they knew what to expect. They waited, the sweat coming out of deep-sunken eyes, rolling down swollen faces on to vulture-like necks, to glisten on emaciated bodies. It was about seven o'clock at night when Lagerführer Karl Fritzsch, Commandant Höss' deputy, and Rapportführer Gerhard Palitzsch, head of the dreaded Political Department, inspected the silent rows of men. The officers' stiff hats carried the death's head insignia of the Gestapo, revolvers were stuck in their belts, and they wore shining black riding boots. Their records were abominable. Fritzsch was responsible, in the absence of Höss, for the first mass murder of prisoners by gas, Cyklon B, used previously for destroying vermin; and Palitzsch boasted he had personally shot 25,000 prisoners and he sought every chance for experimental and novel forms of torture.

One of the prisoners cried, 'My poor wife and children!' It sounded strange and hopeless in that parade-ground, empty of any charity. A fellow-prisoner, Franciszek Włodarski, who was standing only two men away from Kolbe, described the scene, 'Fritzsch and the SS guards walked along one line of ten prisoners and chose one man for the bunker. This line then moved ten steps forwards and the Nazis chose a man from the next line and so on . . .' When Franciszek Gajown-iczek, a Polish sergeant, was singled out he shouted in despair and Włodarski recorded that some of the others who had been selected also cried out. Suddenly a slight figure stepped out of line, took off his cap and moved with halting gait to stand at attention before the SS. He had a flushed face, sunken eyes and cheeks and wore round glasses in wire frames. Prisoners craned to see, because although forlorn cries were not uncommon, no one had ever dared to break rank. It was probably

111

because it was something incomprehensible that Kolbe was not shot where he stood. Fritzsch, who had never before had conversation with a prisoner, asked 'What does this Polish pig want? Who are you?' Kolbe replied, 'I am a Catholic priest. I want to die for that man; I am old; he has a wife and children.' The priest gave a shrewd answer which took account of the Germans' philosophy, to liquidate as priority the old and the weak. Fritzsch signalled Sergeant Gajowniczek to return to his place in the line and Palitzsch, without a sign of emotion, changed the numbers on his list. While the sun set in beauty over Auschwitz the condemned men were drived into the bunker naked and humiliated and afraid. In Cell 18 they were devoid of any dignity in death, naked on the cement floor in the dark subterranean cellars, but they were shepherded by a priest who went with them to die and to help them to die. Father Kolbe took charge of his suffering flock and filled their last days with prayer and psalms. Men in the next cells joined in the praise and supplication. A well-known Polish writer, Jan Józef Szczepański, evoked the awful drama in these words, 'The dying tissue of human solidarity started to pulse with new life . . . Life bought by death again had its value and this long agony of dying became an act of reverence and respect.' It was not, as the Nazis intended, a death of 'undesirables', men who had ceased to be human and had been trampled upon like worms: death in that bleak place was transformed into a celebration. 'Fritzsch', wrote Szczepánski, 'was too narrow in his thinking to perceive that the world of violence was lost by this one act.'

There were only four alive after two weeks and of these men only Kolbe was fully conscious. The authorities became impatient and ordered Hans Bock, head of the hospital barracks, to inject phenol into the priest's veins. Bock was a German criminal in charge of the camp hospital from the beginning, and unlike most of the 'trusties' was kind-hearted, brave and caring, and it is certain that he did what he had to do with gentleness. Father Kolbe was alone at the moment of his death: 12.50 p.m. on 14 August 1941, the Vigil of the Assumption. He was forty-seven years old.

The orderly, Bruno Borgowiec, removed Kolbe's body from the bunker. His job had been to carry out the corpses from that stygian bunker where Father Kolbe held his last sung Mass. 'Sometimes I had the impression that I was in church', he said. The orders of the SS that they were to stop their praying had no effect. Some among the prisoners would beg for a drop of water: the only answer was a kick in the groin. Borgowiec remarked, 'Father Kolbe looking at somebody seemed to be looking through him; the SS couldn't stand that and shouted at him, "Look down, not at us!"'

Friends tried in vain to prevent Father Kolbe's body from being burned. The only concession they won was a wooden coffin and in it his body was put into one of the crematoria that smoked ceaselessly, and afterwards his ashes were scattered. Another witness and fellow priest, Konrad Szweda said, 'I think he would have wished it so for his love was not bounded by place or time.'

CHAPTER TEN

While Maksymilian Kolbe and the other nine men were starving to death, fellow-priests and friends in the camp prayed for the escaper to be caught in the naive belief that the condemned men would then be freed from the bunker and the returned prisoner executed.

Unaware of Maksymilian's death sentence Marianna Kolbe prayed, perhaps more properly, for God's will to be done. She had written to Niepokalanów a few months earlier with plain old-fashioned piety, 'I would give my life willingly to release my son, but while praying I heard an inner voice telling me not to press my own will on God and beg for his freedom, but only to ask for what he needed most to sanctify his soul, and what would be best for the glory of God.' Broken-heartedly, she obeyed this inner voice. 'I pray now that he has the spiritual power stronger than death . . . I pray as a mother who loves her children but believes that their eternal happiness should be valued more than maternal love.'

Official notification of Father Kolbe's death did not reach the Community for five months. It came by post from the German authorities on 24 January 1942. The brothers, however, knew much sooner from one of their own fraternity in the camp. Brother Ferdynand Kasz, whom I met at Niepokalanów, sent them the news in the form of 'an enigmatic history' which was perfectly understood. Brother Cornelius also learnt the news sooner. He was an inmate at Dachau working on a farm when he overheard new prisoners transferred from Auschwitz, whom he recognized as priests (at Dachau all priests wore special numbers to identify their calling) talking about it. He approached one of them and the

114

priest embraced him. 'It is true, your Guardian is dead.' Brother Cornelius told me simply, 'I was at once proud and sad.'

Brother Rufin, Father Kolbe's personal secretary, wrote to Mrs Kolbe, and in October 1941 Brother Gabriel visited her in the convent at Cracow where she acted as lodgekeeper. 'I knew that my son would die a martyr', she told him, and for the first time she revealed the story of Rajmund's vision of the Virgin Mary when a young boy in Pabianice. Of her son's time as prisoner she said, 'I suffered most when he could not attend Holy Mass or take communion.' This was Marianna, the pious Catholic. Marianna the mother said it was not knowing, the lack of news, which had been the worst part, for distress mounts in the darkness. Her one and only letter from Maksymilian had been on 15 June. 'I wish we knew something about his last hours', she said. I read the faithful account of Brother Gabriel's meeting with the saint's mother, filed in the friary's archives, and knew a little rush of pity as momentarily she showed her inmost feelings and admitted jealousy of those spared such pain. But at once she recognized such emotions as temptations and was confident that the work of Niepokalanów, created by her son, would continue under the protection of the Immaculate. She told Brother Gabriel, 'My proper name now is Matka Bolesna (Mother Dolorosa).'

The same sad autumn she claimed a vision of Maksymilian and told one of the brothers about it five years later. She had awoken early but did not rise at once, when suddenly she saw her son in his habit passing slowly before her. He said, 'I always asked you not to worry about me, mother, and now I am very happy.' Marianna repeated three times to Brother Cherubin, 'It was not a dream, it was my son.'

With a little of Maksymilian's prescience, Marianna foretold her own death which happened, as she predicted, on the streets of Cracow in the shade of the cathedral on 17 March 1946. She fell down suffering a heart attack and was heard to murmur, 'O my son.' Her dearest wish was granted for she was buried in a nun's habit. Later the Franciscans wanted to

115

take her body to Niepokalanów, but there was no way of finding where she lay for the coffins were not marked and she was buried in the common grave of the nuns. At the time of her son's beatification in 1971, the whole ground was adorned with flowers.

In the cemetery at Niepokalanów beneath a modern bronze crucifix there is a small urn of ashes taken from Auschwitz to represent vicariously the Father Founder. The body of Maksymilian's younger brother, Alphonsus Kolbe, who died from appendicitis in a Warsaw hospital, also lies here alongside graves of friars killed in the war. The cemetery is carefully tended: every spring fruit trees provide a paean of blossom and flowers are planted freshly as the seasons turn.

Brother Ferdynand, who managed to send early news of Kolbe's death to Niepokalanów, was one of the first to interview Franciszek Gajowniczek when he was freed, and one of the official witnesses of his testament made under oath to the Church. After the war Gajowniczek worked for some years as a civil servant and now he lives on a pension from the Army. He never refuses to do anything the Church asks of him. Often the fathers advise him to take more thought for himself, especially in severe weather; but, said Brother Ferdynand, 'Whenever he is wanted he always comes, to every meeting, procession, Mass. And he even pays his own expenses.'

Brother Ferdynand is a voluble fast-talking man who scolded me for interrupting with supplementary questions; he wanted to recall events in order in his own time. He admires Franciszek Gajowniczek's utter integrity. 'At the beatification many newspapermen came here, and of course, wanted his story and proposed a lot of money. He would never take any money; he was not looking for reward. There were others who offered him money to talk about the treatment meted out to Jews in the camp. Many Polish emigrants in Canada and the USA gave him little presents out of affection for a fellow-countryman, but that was different. He had not got the price

116

of his ticket to Rome for the beatification and the friary bought it for him. Otherwise he will take nothing.'

I asked Brother Ferdynand if Gajowniczek saw himself as a kind of ambassador for the Church. The word was ill-chosen. 'An ambassador conveys a sense of importance. There is nothing self-important about him, he is just accustomed to speaking to people. He is a tough unsentimental man, a professional soldier who has fought many bloody battles and won medals for bravery in two world wars. Now he always ends his speeches, "No more wars, no more cruelties." ' Brother Ferdynand repeated, 'He never turns away any opportunity, never refuses anyone who wants him to talk about Father Kolbe.' I took encouragement and sent a telegram asking to see him. His reply was immediate and brisk, 'Come 11.00 Wednesday Brzeg Gajowniczek.'

Brzeg is a town in Lower Silesia, now in the Opole Province in south-west Poland. My interpreter and I baulked at the friars' stoical suggestion that we take a train which would get us there at three in the morning. Instead, after breakfast, we flew to Wrocław, Poland's third city (formerly Breslau) and took a taxi to Brzeg some forty kilometres to the south-east. We turned into a peaceful leafy street where Franciszek and Helena Gajowniczek live in an old-fashioned gabled house with a pretty if haphazard garden. A picture of Father Kolbe in prison garb hung on the wall, evoking a world of hate and violence remote from the cosy little sitting-room. A sweet smell of lilac drifted through the open window and any connection between that brutal camp scene and the homely old couple seemed fantasy. Helena Gajowniczek, a small motherly woman who yet impresses with a strength of will at odds with her appearance, sat quietly while her husband told his story. Once or twice she tried to interpolate some remarks only to be hushed firmly by Franciszek, a well-built man of strong features and presence. He wore a row of ribbons and his voice was calm as he told his story with a strange mixture of pragmatism and awe.

117

A country lad, he was born on 15 November 1901, in a village called Strachomin, near Mińsk Mazowiecki, in the county of Warsaw. His parents, Jan and Marianna, never sat down to breakfast before saying prayers and the home was enveloped in a religious atmosphere. To use his own words, 'I was born religious and I will die religious . . . My mother brought me up that way and I will remain that way.' From boyhood he longed to be a soldier and at seventeen his ambition was realized when he joined the Army. His first major campaign was The Miracle of the Vistula in 1920 which saved newly-freed Poland from fresh domination by Soviet Russia. Later in the Second World War he went to the front as a sergeant in charge of a unit of university students, and was to gain seven medals. He fought in many battles over the south-west of the country before capture at the Siege of Modlin on 28 September 1939, the same day as Warsaw fell. Modlin (in Russian Poland, 1815–1919, called Navogeorgievsk) lies thirty-two kilometres north-west of Warsaw, and was the site of a strong fortress built by Napoleon. Orders were to surrender the garrison to the Germans for there was no ammunition nor any supplies. All the soldiers were taken prisoners-of-war and split into two sections: officers were to be taken to Działdowo camp in the county of Olsztyn, north of Warsaw; and other ranks to Mława camp, an ancient city also north of the capital. Under cover of darkness some of the prisoners escaped, either singly or in twos and threes. Franciszek made a dash on his own, finding his way to Warsaw to see Helena and their two young sons, Bogdan and Juliusz. There he joined the *Arma Krajowa* (AK), the Home Army, and was sent on a secret mission to the south where he was arrested on the Czechoslovakian frontier. Some three hundred were arrested, betrayed by a spy who had infiltrated the AK. Gajowniczek was imprisoned at first at Zakopane in the Tatra mountains and then, on 8 September 1940, he was sent to Auschwitz as a political prisoner because of his work with the Underground. There were only Poles in the camp for the first year of its existence. He knew that Father Kolbe was the

Guardian of Niepokalanów and he used to read *Rycerz Nie-pokalanej*, but he saw him for the first time at Auschwitz when they were in the same block, No. 14. 'I met him often because he was a father to us all', said Gajowniczek, 'but I did not know him personally.' Kolbe gave religious consolation, heard confessions, and broke his ration of bread for Holy Communion. When the capos left the block, the men used to gather behind the beds and he would move among them. There was no time for a personal conversation with him – 'all were suffering, dying; dead bodies lay everywhere.'

During harvesting in the last days of July, one of his fellow-prisoners in the block saw an opportunity to run away. Escapes from Auschwitz were more common than from camps in German-speaking territory; more than six hundred attempted escape, of whom about a third succeeded. Gajowniczek said charitably that this escaper might not have realized such a terrible reprisal would result. He described the selection for the starvation bunker. 'Father Kolbe was standing four or five men away from me. I cried out something about my poor wife and children, and he stepped out of line and asked Lagerführer Fritzsch if he could take my place. He even tried to kiss the German's hand. It was the greatest miracle for he could have been trampled under foot or shot on the spot . . . It is difficult for me to express my feelings at that moment. I had been sentenced to death and someone had offered his life for mine of his own free will. Was I dreaming? Was it true?' Later he felt conscience-stricken that a holy man had died in his place. The thought obsessed him for a long time and at first he could not talk about it. He tried to hide himself away in bouts of depression. He suffered a strange sort of moral breakdown. But his fellow prisoners consoled him saying that it must have been an act of providence that such an exchange had been allowed, and in Franciszek the conviction grew that he had been singled out to give witness to this heroic deed. Poland needed a saint and his role became clear: he must become a missioner; he must survive to tell the world.

119

The SS harried him after Kolbe's sacrifice for they felt cheated by Gajowniczek continuing to live. His number had been written down but it seemed that he had swindled the system. They scorned Lagerführer Fritzsch and said he must have been out of his mind to accept the exchange: ten men had been selected for the bunker and he should simply have made it eleven. The Lagerführer was a fool. Gajowniczek had been reprieved but later he contracted typhoid and this was equivalent to a death-sentence. He was to be sent to the gas chambers in the morning for he ran a high fever and was useless for work, but the camp Resistance came to his aid and Dr Dering, a camp doctor, was asked to try to save him. He gave Gajowniczek injections to banish the fever and hid him from German guards for some ten days. A dead body was put in his place in the hospital bed so that the number of prisoners tallied when the Germans came to count the sick to be taken to be gassed.

Before Auschwitz was evacuated in January 1945, Gajowniczek was taken to Sachsenhausen, near Berlin, and was there until 20 April 1945. On that day all the prisoners were divided into detachments of five hundred, guarded by ten Gestapo. They were escorted to nearby woods where they slept under trees. For two weeks they had nothing to eat except what they found in the forests. When any prisoner flagged or fainted, the SS simply shot him. There were also women prisoners from Ravensbrück. The Germans wanted all of them to die so that none fell into the hands of the Allies, and they planned to reach German ports and put the prisoners onto ships directed to mined waters. The whole route was littered by dead bodies. Out of the five hundred prisoners in Gajowniczek's party, only twenty-three survived. His weight dropped to forty-four kilos (under seven stone). They were eventually discovered by American units who gave them food; however many died when they ate, having been without nourishment for so long. The survivors of this terrible march were taken temporarily to camps in Germany and Franciszek Gajowniczek was on the first transport to Poland which arrived on 11 November 1945.

He suffered severe back pains and was admitted to hospital. When he was X-rayed doctors diagnosed disintegration of the spine and decided an operation was necessary. When he heard the doctors' decision Gajowniczek decided to discharge himself. He asked for his clothes and painfully made his way home. His wife asked him, 'Are you well?' He said with resolution, 'Yes, I'm well', and concealed his pain. 'But I recovered, and nowadays I have no pains. I believe it is due to Father Kolbe's protection that I am well now.'

He told me that his life had been purposeful and he had visited most countries of the world to talk about Father Kolbe's saintliness. 'He gained a victory in the Second World War,' he declared, 'a victory over Nazism and that great criminal, Fritzsch.'

I looked at this upright old man resolutely recalling these events forty years earlier, and asked him tentatively if he ever tired of the interest shown in him, of visitors like me intruding on his privacy? The question made little sense to him; his job was a missionary's, praising the cause of Father Kolbe. 'It is quite natural that I do it.' Life in the camp remained vivid in his memory, and with the Polish love of sayings he added, 'I have everything in my little finger.' People were friendly and eager to listen. In the beginning thousands would come to hear him when the church announced in advance that he would speak. He was an ordinary soldier but he found the words to address people of all occupations – farm-workers, factory hands, journalists, diplomats and important churchmen. What consoles him and gives him happiness is the thought that Father Kolbe's death was not in vain and that he is venerated as a saint of our time.

At the beatification Gajowniczek gave the chalice to the Pope and was the first to receive Holy Communion. There was an audience with the Pope, Paul VI, who knew no Polish but had learned, *Niech będzie pochwalony Jezus Chrystus*! Let Jesus

Christ be praised! And Gajowniczek in turn had mastered the Italian for 'Long Live the Pope!'

When I asked, 'Do you enjoy life?', Franciszek Gajowniczek took time to reply. 'It is difficult to answer because we have lost two beloved sons. There were moments after I returned from the camp when I thought it might have been better if I had died. "Mother" is always reminiscing about one of our sons, there is no day passes without speaking of them. But, of course,' – and he gave a smile which spread across his impressive face – 'life is beautiful.'

He had spent five years, five months and nine days in prison camps. It was an education and a religious experience. He had tried to make the most of the life which was restored to him as a living witness to an act of love which defeated Lagerführer Fritzsch's world of hate.

The sun filled the room and Franciszek got up and with a chuckle wound his clockwork lovebird. It was a bit of fun which terminated the interview. Helena soon had the kettle whistling and spread a white damask cloth over the table. She brought us coffee and cakes which were a rare treat. I saw Franciszek spill a spot of coffee on the beautifully laundered cloth; he gave me an abashed smile and moved his saucer to cover the traces, but he was not quick enough. Helena noticed and scolded him roundly as if he were a naughty small boy. She warmed to my interpreter, a sensitive and sympathetic woman, and confided in her while Franciszek showed me scrapbooks chronicling his travels. Our taxi came, and I gave Helena a carton of Earl Grey tea and Franciszek some Scotch. They at once offered us some of both: I thanked them for their hospitality. I shall always remember them.

Over a cup of tea in a noisy cafeteria in Wrocław I asked my interpreter to tell me Helena's story. I had wanted to ask her myself about the death of her sons but hesitated to cause her pain. I also sensed that she was shy of my tape recorder. This

122

is the account she gave which I wrote down while it was fresh in her memory.

It was no easy war for Helena. She had hard long years of bringing up their sons alone and in poverty and peril. They lived in Praga, a suburb of Warsaw on the east side of the Vistula, in a house full of the military. She sold a gold watch to enable Bogdan to attend technical school to learn car maintenance. She had been told that there were no places but her son's examination papers were exemplary and the principal accepted him. The watch paid for school fees and tools for one term and then he was given free tuition because of his outstanding ability. The younger son, who had a graphic way of relating events, wanted to be a journalist.

It was a tense time for them all. The mother worried about her sons, the boys feared for their mother's safety. On every street was danger because of the *lapanka*. The Germans would barricade a street or square, or halt a tram, and everyone caught would be driven in vans to Skaryszewska Street for selection. Those fit to work would be deported to Germany. Every Pole was a friend and would be on the alert to pass on warnings. It is easy to imagine the mother's anxiety when her sons were not home before curfew. It is not in the nature of boys to be obedient or punctual, even in war-time, and they were brave boys who helped to distribute the underground press. It is easy too, to imagine the boys' sense of panic when their mother was late home. For one way in which she helped to implement the small family budget was to go into the country to buy farm produce to sell in the town at higher prices. She would be punished if discovered, although it was often easy to bribe the German soldiers who would confiscate the food for themselves. Black marketeering carried lighter penalties than political offences which were dealt with by death, torture or imprisonment. So patriots often carried guns, political papers, and underground newspapers, under the pretext of smuggling butter and eggs.

When all the tenants were ordered to leave the house in Praga, it was difficult to find anywhere to live but Helena

123

succeeded in renting a small room on Krochmalna St, a Jewish quarter in the poorer district of Warsaw. She lived there until the Warsaw Uprising when they were sent to Pruszków, in the county of Warsaw south-west of the capital, where there was a temporary camp for refugees (650,000 people went through the camp). Everyone except the old and the young – who were to be dispersed throughout the country – would be deported to Germany for war work. She had dinned it into her younger son – Bogdan was fighting in Warsaw – to make himself look even smaller. He was old enough to work by Nazi standards but fortunately was of small build. 'Come on, crouch down! Bend your knees, make yourself as small as a mouse!' She had made a game of it. It had worked and when the Germans made their selection Juliusz was put into the category to stay in Poland. But she was ordered to work in Germany, and in great distress she ran to a Polish nurse with a Red Cross arm-band and cried, 'You must help me, my husband is in Oświęcim (Auschwitz), my elder son is struggling in Warsaw and my younger son has been taken from me.' The nurse told her that she must make herself look old so that she would be seen as unsuitable to work in the Reich. Helena pulled an old black handkerchief tightly over her head, scrimping back her hair; she tensed her face into a frown and pulled down the corners of her mouth, and shuffled her feet slowly along the ground. She found the darkest corner of the train and looked vacantly, in the way of the senile, into the faces of the German soldiers who scrutin-ized the frightened old people and small children. It was with enormous relief that she found her son on the train. Now they were together again and after a short time managed to return to Rawa Mazowiecka where Helena had some family and friends. It is a small town in central Poland on the Rawka River, some forty kilometres east of Łódź and they were rejoined here by Bogdan. He had won the Cross of the Brave in the Warsaw Uprising in which many teen-aged boys fought. The Uprising began in the summer of 1944 when the Poles rose against the Germans as the Russian armies reached

124

the city's suburbs. There the Russian advance stopped, and after a heroic struggle of sixty-three days in which Warsaw was devastated, the Poles had to give up. Bogdan was awarded his medal for defending a barricade in the city and was fortunate to escape.

On 16 January 1945 Helena left the house in Rawa Mazowiecka on an errand and told the boys to stay at home. While she was out, Russian bombardment began and they decided to run into nearby woods thinking it would be safer, but they were both killed by shells in the street. Bogdan was eighteen, Juliusz fifteen.

When her husband returned from Auschwitz Helena could not find a flat in Warsaw and decided to move to the west of Poland to the so-called 'recovered lands' from which the Germans were expelled after the last war. Franciszek at first wanted to live quietly and take time to recover from his experiences. He wished to return to his home village but she was adamant that they should have a home of their own. So they settled in Brzeg. The town, where there are the remains of a thirteenth-century Franciscan friary and a castle and church built in the same period, suffered heavy damage in the war. There were few people, empty houses and neglected land.

Hans Frank, aged forty-six, Governor General, alias 'The Butcher' of Poland, was sentenced to death on 1 October 1946 at Nuremberg. He was found guilty on two counts: war crimes, and crimes against humanity; and was hanged at night fifteen days later. The sentences on the leaders of the infamous Third Reich were carried out in the seamy prison gymnasium with its glaring lights focused on three scaffolds, and the sordid legend blazoned on a wall, 'VD Walks the Streets'.

Rudolf Höss, forty-seven, was commandant of Auschwitz from its beginnings until November 1943 when he was transferred to the Berlin Central Office to fill a top job in the Inspectorate of Concentration Camps. In this role he returned to Auschwitz to conduct the 'Aktion Höss' – mass murders of Hungarian Jews in the gas chambers of Birkenau, a sub-camp of the main complex. After the war Höss went into hiding, using the name of Franz Lang, and worked as a farmer in the British zone of occupation where he was recognized and arrested on 11 February 1946. After he was allowed to appear as a defence witness at the Nuremberg trials he was extradited to Polish authorities. In the year Höss spent in the Polish prison (May 1946 to April 1947) he wrote his reminiscences. Of his own position there is evasiveness and self-delusion. He complains, for example, that he was often castigated for obeying the Führer. It had even been suggested that he might have assassinated Himmler. Höss wrote ingenuously, 'I do not believe that of all the thousands of SS officers there could have been found a single one capable of such a thought. It was completely impossible.'

With bathos he complained, 'I was no longer happy in Auschwitz once the mass exterminations had begun . . . When at night I stood out there beside the transports or by the gas chambers or the fires, I was often compelled to think of my wife and children (he had five).' He spoke of his regret that he did not devote more time to his family. 'This exaggerated sense of duty has always made life more difficult for me . . . My wife reproached me and said, "You must not think only of the service all the time but of your family too." Yet what did my wife know about all that lay so heavily on my mind? She has never been told.'

Höss, unshaken National Socialist and one-time modest farmer, was sentenced to death on 2 April 1947 by the Supreme National Tribunal in Cracow. On 16 April of the same year he was hanged in the concentration camp Auschwitz-Birkenau privately for fear of public lynching. He died near the place that was home to him, where his wife wore the silken lingerie of gassed Jews, and their children the clothes of children murdered by his orders. According to a prisoner employed in the Höss household at Auschwitz, Mrs Höss used to say, 'I want to live here till I die.'

126

The subsequent fate of Höss' deputy, Karl Fritzsch, who permitted Kolbe's sacrifice, is uncertain. The Historical Institute and Museum at Auschwitz cannot say what happened to him, and numerous Jewish researchers have been unable to discover the truth. Some think that he died on the Eastern front, while others believe that he was killed fighting communist partisans.

In 1947 the Polish Government in Warsaw asked the British Government to extradite former camp doctor, Władysław Dering, then in the British Isles, on charges of carrying out experimental operations at Auschwitz. The British Government imprisoned him in Brixton pending an investigation, and after nineteen months he was released because of lack of evidence. Eighteen years later Dering sued American writer Leon Uris for libel. On page 155 of his novel *Exodus* Uris wrote, 'Dr Dering had performed 17,000 experimental operations without anaesthetics.' The libel suit revealed that Dering had performed some eighty operations for the removal of sexual glands which had been burnt by X-rays during previous experiments by SS doctors, and that the numbers of experiments cited by Uris were false. The jury found for Dr Dering but awarded him derisory damages of one halfpenny. Witnesses drawn from across Europe bravely gave evidence.

Yet many survivors say Dering saved their lives in the camp as did the Polish sergeant Gajowniczek, spared from the starvation bunker but smitten by typhoid. Dr Dering died in 1966 of lung cancer.

Hans Mulzer, the evangelical minister who was camp commandant at Ostrzeszów where the friars of Niepokalanów were interned in the winter of 1939, wrote to the Community after the war expressing his sadness at Father Kolbe's death. He told the brothers that Kolbe's gift of a 'miraculous medal' went with him from Poland to Russia and France. He attributed to the medallion his escape from death in the streets of Paris in 1944 when a staff car in which he was travelling was machine-gunned from the air. In 1945 he returned to his parish at Münchberg, Upper Franconia, near Hof, where he spent more than thirty years as a Lutheran pastor. His time was fully occupied with church work, teaching and writing. He retired in 1962 and died in 1979 aged eighty-six.

Upon the outbreak of war in 1939, *Maly Dziennik*, Kolbe's national daily, was suppressed by the German authorities. Its one and only editor, Father Marian Wójcik, crossed the border to Romania accompanied by Prince Drucki-Lubecki, Niepokalanów's benefactor. Father Marian wanted to join the Polish armed forces in France or England, but his Superior had other plans. He was sent to America to organize radio programmes and relief aid for Poland. The Count went with him. Later, helped by the Count, Wójcik ran a Catholic press agency with headquarters in New York and sponsored by the Polish Government in exile.

Father Marian died from a heart attack on 26 August 1956. The Count still lives in America. He was instrumental in organizing the Religious Assistance for Poland organization which still helps the Polish hierarchy in its needs. Prince Drucki-Lubecki was invited to the beatification of Maksymilian Kolbe in Rome as a guest of the Franciscans, but he refused since he did not wish that his presence should in the smallest way detract from the honour due to Father Kolbe.

Two days before the beatification on 17 October 1971, Cardinal Wojtyła, Archbishop of Cracow (now Pope John Paul II) in whose diocese Auschwitz camp was located, met the world's press. He said it was 'a sign of the times' that Father Kolbe should be beatified during the Synod then meeting in Rome whose special purpose was to define the meaning of the priestly ministry. 'He gives a concrete answer, this man of flesh and blood . . . who went all the way in his fidelity to his obligations.' Today's young people knew little about the era of the concentration camps, said the Cardinal, and history books record facts which the imagination has a hard time picturing. Of his persecution one prisoner wrote, 'How I hate them all, for they have taught me how to hate.' 'But Maksymilian Kolbe had won the most arduous of all victories, the victory of love which forgives', the Cardinal declared. 'Is his witness not strikingly relevant today, when love is so often stretched out on a cross, so often cleft in twain? How few there are whose brotherly love does not admit some form of segregation – by race, nation or ideology.'

Kolbe's life, writings and miracles were scrutinized by the Sacred Congregation of Rites, the Pope being the final judge. On 14 June 1971 two miracles were approved, both concerning cures attributed to his intercession. Angelina Testoni, a thirty-six year old Sardinian dressmaker from Turritana, who had been under medical treatment for seven years suffering from tuberculosis, was suddenly cured on 24 July 1949; and a fifty-two year old Italian, Francesco Luciano Ranier from Monte Granario, Piceno, gravely ill with blood poisoning, recovered on 5 August 1950 when no human remedy was thought possible.

The beatification took place only thirty years after death, which is one of the shortest periods in the recent history of the Church for anyone to attain such honour. (St Francis died in 1228 and was canonized two years later but procedures were different.) From early dawn the great Basilica of St Peter filled with the faithful who acclaimed the new 'Blessed' with jubilant Polish hymns. The huge congregation included cardinals, patriarchs, bishops, the Vatican diplomatic corps, delegations from the Polish government and from Germany, thousands of priests and Franciscans from all three Orders. Father Cornelian Dende, director of Father Justin's Rosary Hour, a network radio programme in the USA, organized the American party of more than seven hundred, and a large contingent from England was led by Father John Burdyszek, former director of The Crusade of Mary Immaculate. Franciszek Gajowniczek, then seventy-five, and his wife, present in a place of honour near the altar, were two among two thousand, including thirty-six bishops and two cardinals, who came from Poland. Polish pilgrims also came from across Europe, Canada and Japan.

The first reading was in Polish, taken from the Wisdom of

Solomon in the Apocrypha: the final verse of the passage (ch. 3:1–9) reads, 'They that put their trust in him shall understand the truth: and such as be faithful in love shall abide with him: for grace and mercy is to his saints, and he hath care for his elect.' The second reading in Italian came from the First Letter of John.

Pope Paul VI, with the impressive figure of the Polish Primate, the late Cardinal Stefan Wyszyński, at his side, told the vast concourse that few other processes of beatification had been conducted amid such a wealth of information. 'So close is he to our generation, to the happenings we have all experienced in our time, that we all know about him.' He went on, 'Maksymilian Kolbe was perhaps the brightest and most glittering figure to emerge from the darkness and degradation of the Nazi epoch.' Father Kolbe saw his deed as a logical consequence of his priesthood. 'For is the priest not another Christ? . . . What glory it is for us priests, and what a lesson, to find in Blessed Maksymilian such a splendid example of our mission.'

The Pontiff also spoke of the deep affection that motivated Kolbe's sacrifice. 'He was a true Pole, and as a Polish patriot he was willing to give his life for that of a fellow-countryman . . . his heroic act exemplifies in typical fashion the historic destiny of his nation. Poland had learned how to find in the trials that afflict its national life the consciousness of its unity; its chivalrous mission to achieve liberty through the pride of its sons' and daughters' spontaneous sacrifice, and their readiness to give themselves for each other.'

It was impossible to separate the name of Father Kolbe, his activity or his mission from the name of Mary Immaculate. But there was no need to fear that his enthusiasm for the veneration of Mary would develop into some sort of 'Mariolatry', 'for just as the sun will never be outshone by the moon, neither will the mission of salvation confided to the Church ever be threatened because the Church honours Mary as her exceptional daughter and her spiritual mother.'

In the pastoral introduction to his homily the Pope ex-

130

plained the meaning of the title 'Blessed'. 'The Church recognizes him as an exceptional figure, a man in whom the grace of God and his own soul have so come together to produce a stupendous life . . . The new "Blessed" had the privilege of saying with the apostle Paul: "Be imitators of me, as I am of Christ".'

When Paul VI's successor, Pope John Paul II, visited Poland in 1979, he went to Auschwitz Museum 'as a pilgrim'. 'It was impossible for me not to come here as Pope. It was impossible merely "to visit" Oświęcim. It is necessary to think with fear of how far hatred can go, how far man's destruction of man can go, how far cruelty can go.' In his sermon before a vast rapt audience, the Pope quoted the First Letter of St John (1 John 5:4), 'For whatsoever is born of God overcometh the world, and this is the victory that overcometh the world, even our faith.' He went on, 'A victory through faith and love was won by Maksymilian Kolbe in this place, which was built for the negation of faith, and to trample radically not only on love but on all signs of human dignity, of humanity: a place built in hatred and on contempt for man in the name of a crazed ideology.' He asked, 'Can it be a surprise that the Pope who came to the See of St Peter from the diocese in whose territory is situated Auschwitz camp, should have begun his first Encyclical with the words "Redemptor Hominis", and should have dedicated it to the cause of man . . . to his inalienable rights that can so easily be annihilated by his fellow-men?'

My guide at the camp, who told me about this great Mass, said a Jew came to Auschwitz soon afterwards to whom he gave a copy of the Pope's speech. 'What is it to me?' asked the young man; but he took it, and read it and tears flowed down his face. These were the words which so moved him. 'I kneel on this Golgotha of the modern world, on these tombs, largely nameless like the great tomb of the Unknown Soldier. I kneel before all the inscriptions that come one after another bearing the memory of the victims of Oświęcim in many languages. [Prisoners came from twenty-seven nations, the Poles being the majority.] . . . In particular I pause before the inscription in Hebrew. This awakens the memory of the People whose sons and daughters were intended for total extermination. This People draws its origin from Abraham, our father in faith as was expressed by Paul of Tarsus. The very People who received from God the commandment "Thou shalt not kill" itself experienced in a special measure what is meant by killing. It is not permissible for anyone to pass by this inscription with indifference.'

There were both miracles and ironies in Maksymilian's lifetime which invite attention. Those I met, who have experienced the unreal world of concentration camps, declare it was a miracle that both Gajowniczek and Kolbe were not taken into the bunker. There were those after the war who criticized Gajowniczek for agreeing to exchange, but it appears certain that if he had demurred both men would have died. It was not the time or place for philosophical argument and it was unheard of for Fritzsch to be seen talking to a prisoner. It would have been more in character for the Nazis to send both men to starve for any departure from orders was alien to Nazi mentality. This inflexibility was well known in the camp: for example, Kurt Machel, a Silesian seaman who had been condemned to execution, was coached by Resistance doctors how to feign appendicitis; the Nazis would not permit him to die any other way so an unnecessary operation was performed, time was gained, and in this instance his life saved. Gajowniczek regards his own survival after his reprieve as miraculous; he told me that he felt he was especially protected.

It has been said of Kolbe, a chronically sick man, that his work was his greatest miracle. Certainly, the breadth of his achievements, in the face of exceptional obstacles, was extraordinary. Yet Maksymilian insisted that the work of the 'Knights' must be a flowering of the spiritual life; activity without spiritual foundation he regarded as 'the greatest heresy'. He declared that the proper criterion for advance of the Crusade was development of the soul, and wrote at the start of the last war, 'Even if it came to closing down the activities of Niepokalanów; if all the members of the Militia defected; even if we were scattered like autumn leaves throughout the world – so long as in our souls the ideal of the Militia unfolds, then we can boldly claim, "Niepokalanów is making progress".' Now there are three to four hundred parish Kolbean centres throughout the world and some eighteen principal centres with headquarters in Rome where the international director is Father Giorgio M. Domański.

Seibo no Kishi, Japanese Knights of the Immaculate, occupy a new monastery and printing works rebuilt in 1981 on the original site to mark the fiftieth anniversary of the foundation of Niepokalanów at Nagasaki, and there are numerous branches, now religious communities, in all parts of the country. The province now has about 50 priests and 30 brothers and the Guardian, Father Theresianus Sueyoshi, records a new enthusiasm among young men wishing to join them. (In 1982 there numbered 400,000 Catholics in Japan, .3% of the population of 116 millions.)

The principal activities of the Knights at Nagasaki are publishing and education. The Community publishes religious books as well as magazines and bulletins and there is a high school complex which originated as a minor seminary in Father Kolbe's time. The school today has 160 pupils, among whom are 28 minor seminarians. There is a large Catholic school run by the Friars in Nigawa, near Osaka, where there are 2,000 pupils. Pilgrims come to pray in the new church at Nagasaki and before the grotto of the Madonna of Lourdes. Some of them are in Japan to visit Nagasaki's Peace Park for it was at two minutes past eleven on the morning of 9 August 1945 that an atomic bomb exploded about sixteen hundred feet above the city. The blast and thermal rays which exceeded 300,000 degrees centigrade laid it waste. Nagasaki, which means 'long valley', became known as 'the Valley of the Shadow of Death'. More than 40,000 were killed instantly and thousands more, affected by radiation, died later. Others still survive and suffer. Brother Zeno Zebrowski, one of the 'architects' of both Niepokalanów in Poland and The Garden of the Immaculate in Japan, saw the care of homeless children as the most important task facing the friars after the bomb. He had to beg for the means of supporting the children whom he housed in a number of centres. One of the most famous was called 'The Town of the Ants'. Brother Zeno, renowned for his saying 'I have no time to die!', realized that the children lacked a woman's love, so a female Order of Sisters was founded to help care for the orphans and has flourished. The Japanese were so moved by his devotion to their children that they built a memorial tower in Fuji Rayen in 1979 to remember his infinite love. More than a thousand people contributed to built this monument, and the Japanese government conferred the Order of the Sacred Treasure on him for his distinguished services. At the beatification in Rome in 1971 he was embraced tenderly by Pope Paul VI. On 24 April 1982 Brother Zeno died, aged 90. It was the anniversary of the day he had arrived in Nagasaki with Father Kolbe, fifty-two years previously.

On the other side of the Pacific, America's 'Marytown' was established in 1948 at Crystal Lake, Illinois. One year later it moved to Kenosha, Wisconsin, and in 1979 Libertyville, Illinois, became its home. Father Bernard Geiger, America's national director, reports that the Knights' monthly magazine has a circulation of 35,000, another review regularly prints 29,000 copies, a youth bulletin 2,000; and they also publish books. There is tremendous industry allied with intense devotion. Crusade literature in England is the main work of the National Crusade Centre at Manchester where the priests also preach and organize pilgrimages. The present national director, Father Gerard McCann, says that while there is no recorded membership, their magazine has a circulation of 30,000. His predecessor, Father John Burdyszek, now cares for a Polish Home for the Elderly in Corby. He also runs a parish and looks after a permanent exhibition on the life of Kolbe.

Other countries where the work is developing include Italy, Canada, Australia, New Zealand, South Korea, Holland, Malta, South America, Mexico, Africa, Portugal, Spain, Belgium, Switzerland, France and West Germany.

At Niepokalanów, Poland, in the autumn of 1981, for the first time since printing was suppressed in 1952, *Rycerz Niepokalanej* was published for Polish readers. It was permitted a print of 50,000. Readers were asked to pass round their copies, and a print of 100,000 was expected in 1982. In February 1982 I learnt from Niepokalanów that under martial rule printing has again been suspended after three copies of the magazine appeared, but at Eastertide I heard it would soon reappear.

The spread of the Crusade across the world springs from another miracle, the fashioning of the founder by his visions, although little is known of them, for Father Kolbe was reticent about his revelations: he did not wish to be seen as a man set apart. Marianna Kolbe relates his boyish account of how the Virgin appeared to him in church, holding two crowns; the brothers relate his mystical experience in Japan when heaven was promised him 'in all certainty'; and there are witnesses that Maksymilian foretold the future on several occasions, predicting the post-war boundaries of Poland, and his own death.

Tragic ironies in Maksymilian's life and times make this tender story more poignant. Even the most hardened anti-semites in Poland could not conceive the Final Solution envisaged by Hitler. Faced with this atrocity, many Poles who may have favoured a 'cold pogrom' risked their own lives trying to save Jews from the concentration camps. Only four months after Kolbe died in reprisal for an escaper, the camp authorities were ordered by Berlin to stop applying the principle of collective responsibility for escapes. There had been a reversal in the fortunes of war and every prisoner capable of work was urgently needed for munitions. One reason why Kolbe exchanged places with Prisoner 5659 was that this man had a young family. When the two boys were killed in the

135

Russian offensive of January 1945, it is not hard to imagine the feelings of guilt which engulfed their parents adding to the burden of personal grief. Immediately after Kolbe's deed Franciszek Gajowniczek felt depressed and conscience-stricken; and when he was freed from camp he had a resurgence of despair. What right had he to live when a man of God had died such an appalling death, and in vain, for there had been no family reunion? Was he alive under false pretences? Such thoughts tormented him. Yet his sense of deep purpose returned; he became a man with a mission which has been carried out faithfully in Poland and around the world. To Lagerführer Fritzsch the heroism of Kolbe's sacrifice was madness, and therefore unimportant. One number exchanged for another was inconsequential, for the camp's prisoners were only digits in his book and all were doomed. Maybe this is the rational explanation of the miracle of the bunker. Perhaps Fritzsch accepted only because he believed Gajowniczek would die in the ordinary life of the camp anyway; the prisoners had no future and what meaning could this gesture have for people under sentence of death. Fritzsch was too narrow in his thinking to perceive that this singular act defeated the most sinister purposes of the camps: to prove the ethics of brotherhood a fiction, Judaeo-Christian ideas a lie, and humanitarian doctrines cowardice. For where is humanity when you are fighting for a piece of bread and ordered to beat your brother with a stick?

Maksymilian had told the brothers not to join the Underground for they had other work. Yet in his book on the camp Resistance, Garliński describes secret religious services and other attempts at teaching and learning as a demonstration of protest at the iron ring which the SS had tightened around the prisoners. 'They were a sign of rebellion against the system whose aim was to stupefy and destroy . . . they had great significance for the operation of the Underground movement.' Garliński states that the chronicles of Auschwitz record two instances of the voluntary sacrifice of life to save another. The first was Marian Batko, a physics master at Chorzów Grammar School, who died in place of a former pupil on 27 April 1941, but there is no documentation about this deed; and the second, Father Kolbe. Garliński says he was told that there were other examples of self-sacrifice involving men of different nations, but there is no evidence allowing them to be named. 'These acts of sacrifice had no connection with the Underground but testified to an indomitable spirit of opposition to what was happening in the camp. There would have been no Resistance in Auschwitz without the men and women who had the courage to stand up to violence and oppression and those who were moved by love of their fellowmen to give their own lives.'

The joyful confirmation that Blessed Maksymilian would be canonized in October 1982, during the celebrations of the 800th anniversary of St Francis, came while I wrote. Although canon law requires two further proofs of miracles between the beatification and canonization, Pope John Paul II waived these requirements 'for pastoral and ecclesial motives'. I was told by the Apostolic Nunciature in London: 'This means that the step is being taken for the good of the Church and to the benefit of the people of God. It is felt that it will be an effective "sign" that this holy man is held up in this way as an example to the Church.'

Yet sainthood sometimes isolates the hero from ordinary people. Saint Maksymilian must never become a sentimentalized figure of folklore. There are those who declare that he would be a saint it he had died in bed; but his death in the starvation bunker has a universal and imperishable importance. In the camp everything underwent a distillation so that good and evil were seen in absolute terms. Kolbe's heroic act of love – and similar selfless deeds by others – overcame a world of hate. The story of Maksymilian Kolbe is a drama evocative of the early Church, which crystallizes the Christian challenge of love without limits.

Niech będzie pochwalony Jezus Chrystus!

BIBLIOGRAPHY

Archives, Niepokalanów.

Attwater, Donald, *Martyrs from St. Stephen to John Tung* (Sheed & Ward 1958).

Bar, Gioacchino, *The Death of Blessed Maksymilian Kolbe in the Light of the Canon Law* (Milizia dell' Immacolata, Rome).

Burdyszek, John Maria, o.f.m. Conv., *Crusade of Mary Immaculate in England* (Crusade of Mary Immaculate Press, Manchester).

——*Father Maximilian Kolbe, Fire Enkindled* (London 1954).

Cooper, R. W., *The Nuremberg Trial* (Penguin Books 1947).

Delany, H., *The Miraculous Medal* (Clomore & Reynolds).

Dewar, Diana, *All for Christ* (Oxford University Press 1980).

Domański, Giorgio M., o.f.m. Conv., *The historic data about the life of Fr. Maximilian Kolbe* (Milizia dell'Immacolata, Rome).

——*The Cities of the Immaculate in the World* (Miles Immaculatae 1977).

Domański, Jery M., compiler: tr. Regis N. Barwig, *Kolbe, Maximilian Maria, Maria was his middle name: Day-By-Day With Blessed Maximilian Maria Kolbe* (The Benziger Sisters 1977).

Fisher, H. A. L., *A History of Europe* (Edward Arnold 1936).

Garliński, Jósef, *Fighting Auschwitz* (Fontana/Collins 1976).

Geiger, Bernard M., o.f.m. Conv., *Kolbe's 'Blueprint' for World Unity* (Prow Books 1972).

Historical Encyclopedia of World War II (Facts on File Inc., New York 1980).

Kaczkowska, Maria, *Ojciec Kolbe* (Franciszkanie-Niepokalanów 1980).

Leslie, R. F., ed., *The History of Poland since 1863* (Cambridge University Press 1980). (Multiple authorship; particularly indebted to chapters by Dr Antony Polonsky.)

Lorit, Sergius C., *The Last Days of Maximilian Kolbe* (New City Press, New York 1968 and 1981).

Manteau-Bomamy, H. M., *Immaculate Conception and The Holy Spirit* (Kenosha 1970).

Mason, David, *Who's Who in World War II* (Weidenfeld & Nicolson 1978).

Masseron, A., *The Franciscans* (Burns, Oates & Washbourne 1931).

Młodozeniec, J. M. L., o.f.m. Conv., *I Knew Blessed Maximilian* (AMI Press, Washington, New Jersey, 1971).

Pape, Dorothy, *Captives of the Mighty* (China Inland Mission 1959).

Polonsky, Antony, *Politics in Independent Poland 1921–39* (Oxford University Press 1972).

Reischauer, Edwin O., *Japan, the Story of a Nation* (Duckworth 1970).

Sacred Congregation for the Causes of the Saints.

Taylor, A. J. P., *From Sarajevo to Potsdam* (Thames & Hudson 1974).

Tomlin, E. W. F., *Japan* (Thames & Hudson 1973).

West German Television, *A Portrait of a Priest of The Order of Friars Minor* (1971).

Winowska, Maria, *The Death Camp Proved Him Real* (Prow Books/Franciscan Marytown Press 1971).

Wójcik, Marian, o.f.m. Conv., *Organisation and Life at Niepokalanów* (A report presented to the Inter-Province Conference of The Friars Minor Conventual, Crystal Lake, Illinois, USA, 28 August 1956. Fr Marian died two days earlier).

CRUSADE CENTRES THROUGHOUT THE WORLD

BRAZIL

Jardin da Imaculada, Frades
Franciscanos Conventuais, 77–220
Cidade Ocidental, Goias-Brazil.

FRANCE

Centre for Lourdes pilgrims
La Mission de l'Immaculée, 5 Rue
des Petits-Fosses, 65100 Lourdes

ITALY

International Crusade Centre
Convento dell'Immacolata, Via
Laurentina 450, 00142 Rome

National Centre
Convento 'P. Kolbe', Via San
Teodoro 42, 00186 Rome

Centre for Polish exiles
Convento dell'Immacolata, Via
Guinone Lucina 75, 00050 Santa
Severa, Rome

Convento San Francesco d'Assisi,
Via Crociferi 2, 95124 Catania

Sanctuario S. Maria del buon
consiglio, Frati Minori Conventuali,
83040 Frigento, Piana della Croce
(Avellino).

Convento Piccola Citta
dell'Immacolata, Via Monte Fasce
81, Genova.

	Convento San Francesco, Via del Municipio Vecchio 19, 67069 Tagliacozzo
JAPAN	Seibo no Kishi Friary, 196 Hongochi-cho, Nagasaki-shi, Nagasaki-ken 850
MALTA	St Francis Friary, Tower Rd., St Paul's Bay
NETHERLANDS	Ridderschap der Onbevlekte, Convent S. Lambertus, Driessensstraat 24, 6015 AG – Neeritter.
PHILIPPINES	Franciscan Conventual Church, St Quiteria Church, Caloocan City, Metro-Manila 3108
POLAND	OO Franciszkanie, 96–515 Teresin k-Sochaczewa, Niepokalanów
UK and IRELAND	All Saints Friary, Redclyffe Road, Urmston, Manchester M31 2LE
USA	Our Lady of Fatima Friary, 1600 Park Avenue, Libertyville, Illinois 60048
WEST GERMANY	Minoritenkloster, Kapellengasse 10, D-6700, Ludwigshafen 25
ZAMBIA	Franciscan Centre, PO Box 70992, Ndola

INDEX

145